The
Official History of

BLUE
SKY
MINES

TO
Mrs Pierpont
(aka the lovely and long-suffering Daya)

The Official History of BLUE SKY MINES

TREVOR SYKES

Illustrations by **Ward O'Neill**

THE AUSTRALIAN
FINANCIAL REVIEW

AFR BOOKS

By the same author:

The Money Miners, 1978
Vintage Pierpont, 1985
Two Centuries of Panic, 1988
Operation Dynasty, 1989
The Bold Riders, 1994

A publication of the Financial Review Library
a publishing division of John Fairfax Publications Pty Ltd ACN 003 357 720

The Financial Review Library is a member of Publish Australia

Managing editor: Sarah Hodgkinson
Publishing consultant: Ann Atkinson

Printed in Australia by Pirie Printers Pty Limited, Canberra
Typeset by DOCUPRO, Sydney
Cover illustration: Ward O'Neill
Cover design: Carolyn Wilson, Mango Design Group

Copyright © 1996 in text Trevor Sykes
Copyright © 1996 in illustrations Ward O'Neill

National Library of Australia Cataloguing-in-Publication data

Skyes, Trevor.
  The official history of Blue Sky Mines.

  ISBN 1 86290 116 3.

  1. Australian wit and humor. 2. Mineral industries—Humor.
  3. Speculation—Humor. I. Title.

332.6722

All rights reserved. No part of this publication may be reproduced, stored in a retrieval system, or transmitted in any form or by any means electronic, mechanical, photocopying, recording, or otherwise, without prior written permission of the publisher.

Contents

Foreword vi
Introduction vii

1. IN THE BEGINNING THERE WAS BLUE SKY . . .
Come fly, come fly, a pie in the sky 2; Penwiper's brilliant career 5; As my Daddy said, two's a company 9; Keeping dry in the wet 11; Putting some blue sky into the accounts 15; A clear case of salt 18; Spring — a time not to get sprung 22
TECHNICAL BRIEF 1: The Blue Sky policy on ore reserves 28

2. INTO THE 1980s
In search of a small, credible loss 35; Dancing the three-step contra 38; The year of the dragon 41; An impressionist annual report 44; What bears do in hibernation 46; Getting your priorities right 50; Under analysis 52; Sir Mark lends a hand 58
TECHNICAL BRIEF 2: How to spot a high-risk company 62

3. THE BOOM YEARS
In Blue Sky we trust 69; Caught short with a fistful of dollars 71; Golden pillars of salt 73; What's a few noughts between friends? 76; Blue Sky discovers platinum 81; Playing the Last Card 83; In on the mezzanine floor 86; A few generally accepted principles 90
TECHNICAL BRIEF 3: How to run a mining company 93

4. AFTER THE GREAT CRASH
Just a bit too much capital 99; Blue Sky lays another smokescreen 101; A bit short of Blue Sky 103; Keeping it underground 106; Dear Diary 108; When I'm calling you 112; Who killed Round Robin? 114; Baser and baser 117
TECHNICAL BRIEF 4: How to conduct board meetings 121

5. THE 1990s AND THE RECESSION WE JUST HAD TO HAVE
One-way preference shares 127; Last rites for Last Card 128; The great sacred gin cupboard 132; Getting to the core of the problem 134; Big Goanna falls from Blue Sky 136; A nice place for a placement 139; Following the government's lead 141; Don't worry, this won't hurt a bit 143; An anomaly not quite along the right lines 145; Pierpont strikes gold 147; Hot gravel, well seasoned 151; Total quality comes to Blue Sky 153; Blue Sky's surprise Christmas parcel 156
BACKGROUNDER: Inside the Croesus Club 162

Foreword

*I*t was by no means easy to compile this history of the Blue Sky Mines. The official minutes had been destroyed in three separate fires (all coinciding with investigations of the company) and the few that remained showed signs of tampering. All that was left was contemporary anecdotal evidence.

After their board meetings, the directors of Blue Sky invariably indulged in a long lunch at the Croesus Club. The records of the meetings reproduced here were jotted down by old Pierpont after the lunches, which often did not end until dark. One difficulty is that he rarely emerged from one of these lunches fully sober, making both his memory and handwriting unreliable. Another is that the jottings were frequently on the back of Croesus Club drink coasters and therefore covered with a rich patina of claret stains. And sometimes he was incapable of writing until his hangover cleared days later.

Nevertheless, on the grounds that these are contemporary records of the board's dark deeds spanning two decades, we feel entitled to call them an official history.

INTRODUCTION

Welcome to the world of Blue Sky Mines, where accounting practices and geological standards are stretched to their rubbery limits.

The existence of Blue Sky Mines (No Liability Except at Gunpoint) was first revealed in the Pierpont column of *The Bulletin* of June 6, 1978. Until then the affairs of this mining company had been hidden from the investing world - and for good reason.

Blue Sky is a company run with the deeply criminal intent of separating investors from their money. It is not really a mining company because its directors have no intention of ever starting a mine. However, Blue Sky is always *talking* about starting a mine and sometimes enough innocent or greedy punters buy its shares, not realising that what they are really doing is providing the funds for Pierpont's next Caribbean cruise.

Apart from Pierpont there are four directors of Blue Sky. The chairman, Sir Mark Time, is an old drone from the Croesus Club who was chosen the head the board because he looks respectable and is far too thick to understand the plots and schemes of the other directors. Spender the accountant and Bottle the geologist are renowned for the technical expertise they can bring to the task of defrauding shareholders. And Penwiper the secretary keeps the records of the company meetings - or the directors' highly suspect version of what happened anyway.

As Pierpont penned his tales of Blue Sky in *The Bulletin*, *Australian Business* and now in *The Australian Financial Review*, his little company became something of an institution among Australia's mining and investment fraternity. Some of Pierpont's best story ideas have come from directors of mining companies or stockbrokers who have rung and said: 'Here's an idea for Blue Sky. Have you seen what's happening in so-and-so...'. If the Australian mining game ever became totally pure, Pierpont would run out of ideas. Fortunately, there seems no present danger of that happening.

Blue Sky should not be taken as typical of Australian mining morality. All around the country accountants and geologists have been painstakingly trying to devise new accounting standards and ore reserve statements that will make company reporting more honest. Unfortunately, every time such upright chaps introduce a new concept and it is used by some legitimate company, Blue Sky finds ways of twisting the new standard to its own foul ends.

It might be pointed out that Blue Sky's directors are not only criminal, but incompetent. At various times, they have issued more shares than their authorised capital permitted, they have bungled the salting of their latest assays and they have even printed an annual report containing somebody else's accounts.

Believe it or not, Blue Sky has nevertheless spawned a string of imitators. There was a Blue Sky chain of dress shops, a Blue Sky Mines that was a subsidiary of the mighty Anglo-American Corporation of South Africa and a bald pop singer named Peter Garrett produced an album called *Blue Sky Mining*. Best of all was a literally fly-by-night English outfit called Blue Skies Travel which went broke and left all its customers stranded in Spain.

Two Queensland fans of Pierpont formed a company named Blue Sky Mines which they used as a vendor of a few prospects into Bligh Coal back in the 1980s. The underwriter, drumming up support for the float, rang one little old lady who had actually read the fine print in the prospectus. 'Well, if you recommend these shares, I'll take them,' she said. 'But I'm not sure about this company Blue Sky Mines. They get dreadful write-ups in the papers, you know.'

That's fame.

Welcome to Blue Sky Mines.

IN THE BEGINNING, THERE WAS BLUE SKY ...

The existence of Blue Sky Mines (No Liability Except At Gunpoint) was first revealed by Pierpont on June 6, 1978, in a column entitled 'Come Fly, Come Fly, A Pie in the Sky'.

Last Card was chosen as a scheelite mine because nothing else was particularly exciting at the time.

Uranium mining had been effectively blocked by Malcolm Fraser. Gold was in the doldrums. The US Treasury and the International Monetary Fund had been selling off their gold stocks since 1975 on the basis that gold was no longer a monetary metal. The IMF averaged $US246 an ounce and the US Treasury averaged $US255. Why anybody listens to their economic advice is still a mystery to Pierpont.

But diamonds began to glitter after the Argyle discovery in the Kimberleys, and Blue Sky joined the rush enthusiastically.

In late 1978 the all ordinaries index was 380 and rising. A giant base metal orebody named Macarthur River had been discovered. The metallurgy made it difficult to treat but it was expected to come on stream soon.

The Official History of Blue Sky Mines

The Federal Government had barred sand mining at Fraser Island, even though the joint venture partners, Dillingham and Murphyores, had a valid export licence. Having expropriated the miners, Malcolm Fraser refused to pay them compensation.

Aboriginals threatened the sacred rights of mining companies by declaring a sacred site existing on a spot where an oil well was to be drilled at Noonkanbah in the Kimberleys. The banner of the miners was kept aloft by the Premier of Western Australia, Sir Charles Court, who insisted that the well be drilled despite massive protests and a picket line.

The prices of mining shares were kept aloft by various corporate raiders of the day, most notably Alan Bond and Robert Holmes à Court.

The market was kept honest by the stern vigilance of the Corporate Affairs Commissions run by the state governments.

COME FLY, COME FLY, A PIE IN THE SKY

The directors of Blue Sky Mines No Liability were barely sentient when the extraordinary board meeting began at 9.30 a.m. Pierpont and Bottle the geologist were nursing hangovers and casting sidelong glances at the bar cabinet, but Spender the accountant had just ordered coffee all round.

Penwiper the secretary was easily the most alert, having just finished fabricating the minutes of the last meeting. Sir Mark Time, the chairman, was, as usual, cataleptic.

'Sorry to drag you in so early,' apologised Penwiper, 'but the stock exchange has asked why our shares rose from four cents to 50 in the past week and if we don't reply promptly there's a danger they'll suspend us. They've been in a hanging mood lately.'

'I don't understand,' said Sir Mark. 'We haven't been doing anything recently, have we?'

Pierpont shifted his aching cranium onto his right hand and groped blindly for his cigar case. For once Sir Mark was close to the target, because the whole run had basically been set up three years ago.

Blue Sky had been a typically feverish child of the nickel boom, running an amazing burst of high temperature on the mining boards

In the Beginning, There Was Blue Sky . . .

and then fading away to a shadow. It had been floated on the crest of the 1969-70 wave with nothing except some hastily acquired scrubland in Western Australia and a tight capitalisation.

It had enjoyed a wild market run which had pushed the 10c paid shares over the five-dollar mark on the basis of some nickel assays for which none of the vendors was ever convicted, the largest having left abruptly for Sierra Leone when the investigation started. A fire in the head office the night before had fortuitously wiped out all the company's files.

After that, the market crashed and the shares were half a cent seller with no bid. Then one night in the Croesus Club during late 1974, when Whitlam's Reign of Terror was at its height, Pierpont and Spender put together a game plan. We picked up the vendor shares plus a few more on market, getting about 40 per cent of issued capital on very small outlay. After achieving control, Pierpont and Spender put a call on the contributing shares, forcing out the small shareholders in droves. The number of issued shares dropped dramatically, with Spender and Pierpont controlling 80 per cent of them. Blue Sky was then just within stock exchange requirements on spread of capital.

Blue Sky was still listed, albeit with no assets apart from a million dollars (the call money which Pierpont and Spender had contributed – and promptly borrowed back) and some quite worthless mineral claims. It had been turned into a clean, tightly capitalised shell, and the shares had not been above a few cents until a week ago.

'I don't understand,' repeated Sir Mark. 'Why could the shares have risen?'

Spender decided to reply. 'The shares certainly aren't running on anything in the balance sheet,' he said. 'Net tangible asset backing and earnings are both close to zero.'

That was true enough. Blue Sky had its puny cash on deposit, earning barely enough to pay Penwiper's meagre salary.

Bottle had come to Blue Sky in 1976 with the Last Card scheelite deposit. Like any prospector with a marginal orebody, he had shied away from Australia's mining giants because they were no longer interested in any project worth less than a million dollars and they would have paid him peanuts anyway. Consequently Bottle was looking for a small, desperate company where he could do a deal. Blue

Sky took an option over Last Card and Bottle took an option over the forfeited shares at their fully paid par value of 25c.

So the game had been set up. Pierpont and Spender had 80 per cent of the company, which would be reduced to 40 per cent if Bottle ever exercised his option. Bottle would not exercise until the shares were significantly above 25c and the only way he could get them there was by convincing the market that Last Card was a bonanza.

Penwiper was a shrewd young chap the three of us had picked up to mind the share register, forge minutes of meetings and lose inconvenient documents. We had not told him anything of our plans, but a Hong Kong nominee company had suddenly emerged as a buyer, mopping up small parcels in the market.

The only other thing we needed was an imposing figurehead to sign company releases. Sir Mark Time — one of the legion of old drones inhabiting the Croesus Club — was a former public servant who had been pensioned off with a knighthood because he had been found incompetent even beyond the standards of Canberra. All Blue Sky needed now that the world tungsten price was rising was a favourable assay report. By now, this had even occurred to Sir Mark.

'Is there anything we can report from Last Card?' he asked.

'Well,' said Bottle. 'We've completed preliminary work — not being able to afford a percussion drilling program, as you know — and while it looks favourable, I haven't got any hard figures on it yet. I should have a report to the board in the next fortnight. And our negotiations for a farm-out to Gigantic Mines Inc. of Canada are still open.'

This was true, as far as it went. Blue Sky had not drilled the prospect because many a good mine has been ruined that way. Also, the reason Bottle did not have his report ready was that he was trying to find some way of implying high tungsten grades without mentioning the disturbingly high molybdenum content. In fact, if the impurities rose any higher Last Card would have to become a molybdenum mine, contaminated by traces of tungsten. And the last letter between Blue Sky and Gigantic had been seven months ago, which meant the negotiations were not so much open as forgotten.

'Then why has there been so much turnover in the stock?' asked Sir Mark.

In the Beginning, There Was Blue Sky...

This was the time to display confidence. Pierpont waved an insouciant Tabacalera, nearly suffocating poor Penwiper. 'A little portfolio readjustment by Spender and myself,' Pierpont said gruffly. 'Just putting the scrip into a company with some taxable profits. Have to do it on-market these days or the Corporate Affairs Commission wallahs come around asking questions.'

Once again, not the whole truth. Pierpont and Spender had sent some of their portfolio around in a circle. A series of on-market marriages in Sydney, Brisbane and Melbourne had given the market the impression that a quarter of Blue Sky's shares had turned over in a week. Technically, these are known as 'wash sales', designed to create a spurious picture of activity in a stock.

The massive volume, on price rising from two to four cents, had sucked in the professionals, who had pushed it the rest of the way to half a dollar while Spender and Pierpont had been frantically unloading. So had Bottle, although he had not exercised his option yet and was technically short a quarter of a million shares.

'Well, it seems clear enough to me,' said Sir Mark. 'I suggest we send the exchange a statement saying that we expect a report on Last Card from our geologist in a fortnight, and that we are still negotiating with Gigantic, but other than that we know of no reason for the rise in the share price.'

The motion was passed unanimously.

PENWIPER'S BRILLIANT CAREER

Blue Sky's secretary Penwiper was recruited in the winter of '75, just before balance date, when our previous secretary Sipperley absconded suddenly for Paraguay.

The board issued a statement expressing shock and horror at Sipperley's departure, our grief the more poignant because he was accompanied by the liquid assets. But as the statute of limitations must have expired on the whole affair by now, Pierpont can tell you that the board was not too surprised at all. Indeed, the whole defalcation had taken more negotiation than the SALT treaty.

You see, '75 had been a bad year for the directors. We had sunk rather a lot of money into Cambridge Credit shares on the premise that it couldn't possibly be as badly run as the rumours were saying.

The Official History of Blue Sky Mines

When this proved wrong, we were forced to cover our contract notes by robbing Blue Sky.

The hole in our accounts was so large that even the creative genius of Blue Sky's directors had been unable to find a way of papering it over, and by mid-June we were all starting to check airline schedules. Then Spender approached Pierpont at the Croesus Club one day and whispered: 'I think I've found the way out.'

'I knew the accountancy profession wouldn't let me down,' Pierpont sighed with relief. 'You've found some starkly insane standard that will enable us to show our liabilities as assets?'

'Not this time,' Spender smiled, showing just the tips of his teeth. 'I've discovered our secretary has been pilfering. He's taken us for about 15K with false invoices.'

In terms of detective work, Pierpont should point out that this was a little short of Sherlock Holmes' league. As Blue Sky never spends any money on mining, it has no trade creditors. The only invoices ever submitted are falsified expense claims by the directors. The appearance of an invoice that was not one of our own was akin to having a stranger appear at the family breakfast table one morning. It stood out, if Pierpont makes his meaning clear.

In the Beginning, There Was Blue Sky . . .

'Well, we could have him arrested,' muttered Pierpont. 'But I don't think we should be drawing the attention of the constabulary to our finances right now.'

'You're on the wrong track,' Spender murmured, his teeth looking sharper. 'I was thinking of encouraging him.'

'I see,' Pierpont grinned, for the first time all June. 'Have a glass of Bollinger.'

The negotiation was speedy, but intense. The board agreed to turn a blind eye while the secretary embezzled $107,239.62, which was all the money left in Blue Sky. We also provided a free one-way ticket to Paraguay where, fortunately, the chap had some distant relatives from the old Utopian settlement.

In return, he wrote a heartrending confession that he had taken all the missing funds ($1,107,239.62) and could not face the shame and humiliation of telling us personally. The financial details were fairly easy to settle, but we had to spend a week persuading him that Paraguay was preferable to Pentridge – Alexander Barton having given it a bad name at the time. Even as Spender was pushing him through the embarkation gate at Tullamarine, the chap seemed to be having second thoughts.

We now had an explanation for the missing money. All we needed was a new secretary, so Blue Sky advertised. Which meant that a week later Pierpont and Spender were sitting in the boardroom screening applicants.

The first applicant almost ran through the door. He was an eager beaver with a shiny new MBA and a rabid enthusiasm for Total Quality Management. He spent half an hour extolling the virtues of TQM and what it could do for Blue Sky before Pierpont could get a word in edgeways.

'Do you know how many staff Blue Sky has to manage?' your correspondent asked.

'No,' replied the MBA, pausing for breath.

'One,' Spender informed him. 'The secretary.'

'That's great,' he burbled.

'You've rationalised staff already. I can see I'm among people who are receptive to modern management systems.' Bottle the geologist, who had been retained for the day as bouncer, threw him out into the street before he could waste any more of our time.

The second applicant was even worse, being a computer freak. He fixed us with a glittering eye like the Ancient Mariner and babbled to us about spreadsheets and e-mail and networking.

Bottle fell into a trance until the freak said his computers could be used to collate exploration data and get an instantly accurate evaluation of an orebody. He was out in the street before he completed the next sentence.

The last applicant was Penwiper, who shuffled in thin-faced and nervous. He perched on the edge of his chair, fumbling with his tie as Pierpont pretended to re-read the CV he had sent us.

Pierpont waited until a few beads of perspiration had appeared on Penwiper's brow before saying: 'I see you got Honours at Melbourne in '72?'

'Yes, sir,' said Penwiper, running a finger around his collar.

'That was jolly good going, considering they expelled you in '71 after the squash club funds disappeared,' mused Pierpont.

'What, sir?' gasped Penwiper, startled.

'The vice-chancellor's an old friend of mine and I had a chat with him about you last night,' your correspondent explained. 'Discreetly, you'll be glad to know.'

'I can explain that,' croaked Penwiper. 'I needed to cover a small deficit in my investment portfolio . . .'

'But they expelled you from University at the time, so that leaves a small gap in your CV in '72,' Pierpont said.

Bottle intervened. 'That would have been when you were doing the short stretch on French Island?'

Penwiper choked a bit. 'But how did you know that?' he croaked, finding speech at last.

'Friend of mine in the Prisons Department,' explained Bottle. 'Shoplifting, wasn't it?'

Penwiper was trembling. 'That was different, sir,' he croaked again. 'My fiancée wanted a rather expensive engagement ring . . .'

Spender cut him off. 'What I liked best about your accountancy certificate was the signature of the institute's president,' he said admiringly. 'I'm one of his best friends and I'd never have picked it as a forgery if I hadn't checked with him about your qualifications. Also discreetly, you'll be glad to know.'

Penwiper opened his mouth but no sound emerged. His face had gone a pretty ash-grey.

'In my years as a director I've kept some pretty rough company at times,' said Spender. 'But this is the first time I've run across anyone who could have been criminally convicted on his CV alone. But you'll be glad to know we're understanding fellows.'

'Sir?'

'We're actually looking for someone who'll take a broad view of company practices. We'll help you, if you'll help us.'

Comprehension began to dawn on Penwiper. He took a deep breath and said: 'I'm sure I can meet whatever requirements you have, sir.'

Spender raised an eyebrow in Pierpont's direction. Pierpont nodded.

'Our first requirement relates to your predecessor,' said Spender. 'He's just fled the country with $1.1 million. We can prove the one hundred, but we need a paper trail to prove he took the one million as well.'

Penwiper smiled for the first time. 'That should only take a couple of days, sir,' he said. 'I'll start tonight.'

At that point Sir Mark Time bumbled into the room.

'This is our new man, Penwiper,' said Pierpont. 'Keen young chap. He's already unravelling the mess left by our last secretary.'

'How frightfully efficient,' beamed Sir Mark. 'Next thing you know he'll be balancing our accounts.'

'That's not really my field,' smiled Penwiper.

'But I might be able to help with the audit certificate.'

AS MY DADDY SAID, TWO'S A COMPANY

Marriage, of course, is primarily designed as an income-splitting device.

Wives are very useful for forming companies, acting as public officers, signing annual returns and holding B class shares. Any other dividends to be derived from the ladies are strictly fringe benefits.

That, in any case, is how Pierpont's father explained it all in the heart-to-heart chat they had when your correspondent was eleven.

Pierpont's own marriage was a deeply romantic affair, which stirred the bank balances of both families. It brought a string of coal mines into conjunction with a railway network in a sublime moment of vertical integration.

On that foundation, Pierpont and his bride have built a deep and lasting relationship. She has her bridge clubs and luxury cruises while Pierpont has the Croesus Club and Flemington. Your correspondent and Mrs Pierpont meet every Sunday at their country estate to countersign dividend cheques.

In the course of this happy union, three progeny have been produced to act as junior partners in the family trust.

It's a love story straight out of the women's magazines, as all Pierpont's colleagues admit. Pierpont and his bride have been co-directors of the family company for nigh on 60 summers now, stripping trusts and opening Swiss bank accounts together.

This connubial idyll has now entered a new dimension as Pierpont has turned his wife into a prospector.

A few months ago, Pierpont and his geriatric cronies were manipulating the shares of Blue Sky Mines No Liability on the strength of a quite hopeless tungsten mine. We ramped the shares, but then they fell into the doldrums and ever since we had been looking for a new mineral syndicate to stir a few rumours in the financial fraternity.

Which is where the Carat Syndicate comes in. This syndicate is pretty well all Mrs Pierpont, apart from a few bemused Kimberley pastoralists and an industrial chemist.

Pierpont is fairly sure he knows where the action will be in the coming boom. Whatever other glamour stocks run, diamond miners will be among them.

Your correspondent was talking the other day to a mining company promoter who holds diamond claims over half of the Kimberleys and he showed your correspondent some photographs of potential diamond pipes. From the air they looked like big circular patches, sometimes with a blue tinge.

Armed with this new-found technical expertise, Pierpont organised the formation of the Carat Syndicate. This syndicate is now busily pegging all the racetracks in the Kimberleys. These are flat and roughly circular and as soon as the next dry season starts in about

In the Beginning, There Was Blue Sky . . .

April the industrial chemist is going to manufacture large quantities of blue paint.

A few aerial photographs will be taken of the blue race tracks and then the Carat Syndicate will suddenly bob up as a vendor to Blue Sky Mines. Mrs Pierpont has agreed to the whole scheme as long as she doesn't have to go anywhere within a thousand kilometres of the Kimberleys.

The only drawback is that Pierpont will have to cut the Blue Sky secretary, young Penwiper, and his fellow directors, Bottle and Spender, in on the deal. The four of us have a gentleman's (to use the term loosely) agreement that we are not allowed to rip off Blue Sky unless we do it together.

Meanwhile we should be able to put out a few bearish statements about Blue Sky's existing assets to shake the speculators out of the stock and enable us to soak up a few shares at low prices on market before we ramp them again.

It's really just a little harmless pastime and it keeps Pierpont off the streets.

In the words of Mae West: 'Diamonds is my career.'

KEEPING DRY IN THE WET

When the board of Blue Sky Mines meets these days, the directors do not fritter away their precious time talking about the company's mineral prospects.

The company's mineral prospects being what they are, the less said about them the better. No, we spend our time discussing the share market, and we know of no more enjoyable subject of conversation.

The long rise across the boards since late 1978 have made us all a great deal richer. We are naturally pleased with this, but we are even more pleased with our display of investment acuity, which marks us as the owners of superior intellects.

It occurred to Pierpont at the last meeting, however, that the directors had achieved success by a remarkable variety of methods.

Take that old dunderhead, Sir Mark Time, who was chosen as Blue Sky's chairman precisely because he knew nothing about either mining or the share market. Sir Mark has been spectacularly success-

11

ful over the past year because he's been buying shares in a vertically integrated miner called Broken Hill Proprietary Co Ltd.

Sir Mark is easily the biggest winner in the Blue Sky stable. He was buying BHP all through the first quarter of 1978 and is now showing huge profits. Readers have probably forgotten, but BHP hit a low of $5.16 a share in February 1978 and did not rise above $6 until the end of March. As Pierpont writes, the stock is hovering around the $11.50 mark and analysts are talking about it running to $15. On numbers, therefore, Sir Mark is a genius.

The drawback is that Sir Mark has one of those brains that are capable of holding only one idea at a time. When it comes to investment, his sole idea is that BHP is a good company and must therefore be a good investment. He has been a steadfast admirer of BHP sine the young Essington Lewis was boiling zinc ore at the Barrier. He bought the stock all the way up to $25 in 1968 and all the way down again. He would doubtless continue buying whether BHP struck another Saudi Arabia, appointed Muhammed Ali chairman or went bankrupt.

Spender the accountant has also been buying BHP, but characteristically in a more devious fashion. He has been doing buy-and-writes, buying the shares on market, then writing them

In the Beginning, There Was Blue Sky . . .

against three-month and six-month traded options. On the bull market since November this has been virtually a foolproof way of making money.

At present Spender is buying BHP on market at $11.50 and simultaneously writing options to deliver the stock in June at $11. On the surface this may appear suicidal, but the premium is $1.35 and this goes to Spender. If BHP goes to $13, Spender delivers the scrip and pockets his $1.35, which includes 85c profit less the interest on any borrowings. If the price goes to $11, the buyer of the option spins a coin, but whatever happens Spender won't lose. He may also fatten his profits by picking up BHP's final year dividend into the bargain.

Spender reckons he is averaging a return of 15 per cent on BHP through this mechanism. The difference between his strategy and Sir Mark's is fundamental. Sir Mark buys BHP taking the full risk of any fall and reaping the full advantage of any gain. Spender almost eliminates the risk of loss in return for a percentage profit.

Spender never buys anything without simultaneously selling it. He misses the big profits but he will never finish in chancery. His main problem is staying liquid, because when he goes long he sometimes runs out of money and has to pilfer the Blue Sky petty cash to keep eating. Given the usual state of Blue Sky's petty cash, this is an excellent way of dieting.

Bottle the prospector is an avowed and dedicated inside trader. He would not dream of investing in a share unless he knew something important about the company which had not yet been disclosed to the public at large.

Whenever he hears, through the geologists' mafia, that Bloggs Mining or whoever is buying a hot uranium prospect, he buys a few thousand shares. This technique has served him well over the past few months because all his shares have been galloping ahead handsomely.

The technique has a couple of flaws. The most obvious is that if the Corporate Affairs Commission ever discovers what Bottle is doing he will be flung into a dungeon and quite probably executed by their firing squad. Any CAC sleuth tracking Bottle, however, will first have to unravel a maze of nominee companies in obscure tax havens, notably Bermuda. Bottle calculates that on the standard expense

13

allowance granted by the CAC, no sleuth will ever be able to afford to stay in Bermuda, Jersey, Panama and the rest for long enough to do all the unravelling.

The less obvious hazard is that insider knowledge does not guarantee success. When Bloggs Mining ultimately announces its acquisition of the uranium prospect, it may be on the day that the Movement Against Uranium Mining is throwing Molotov cocktails at the yellowcake shipments from Ranger.

Also, working on insider information means that Bottle is concentrating on the more or less legitimate small exploration companies. In Pierpont's experience, legitimacy is a serious handicap to any explorer's share price in a really hot boom, but we have not yet arrived at those conditions in the current market.

Blue Sky's young secretary Penwiper joined the company poor, a condition he has since been trying strenuously to amend. He was so young he thought the market could best be conquered by a strictly rational approach, so he began studying theses on the subject and predictably became convinced by random walk theory. In very broad terms, this postulates that you might as well pick stocks with a pin, which is what Penwiper did.

At his New Year's Eve party, Penwiper pinned the stock exchange quotations to the rumpus room wall and threw darts at it to pick six companies. To ensure that his subconscious did not take over and begin aiming for selected stocks, he painstakingly inebriated himself first and then stood the length of the room away from his target.

If he had followed all the recommendations discovered by the darts, his investments would have included seven floorboards, two roof beams, three light bulbs and his wife's right ear lobe. However, he also managed to hit six stocks. They were Halmac Services Ltd, Trio Insulations (Holdings) Ltd, Rover Hotels Ltd, Marra Developments Ltd, Katanning Holdings Ltd and MIM Holdings Ltd.

Any security analyst who had put this lot together as a recommended portfolio would probably have been tarred and feathered – not to mention receiving a reference to the nearest good psychiatric hospital – but it has performed remarkably well.

Katanning is almost never traded, so Penwiper was unable to get set. Of the rest, Halmac has made it from $1 to $1.30, Trio from $1.70 to $1.85, Rover from 90c to 96c and MIM – star of the show

In the Beginning, There Was Blue Sky . . .

— from $2.46 to $3.30. Marra Developments, which Pierpont would have bought only if the alternative was torture by hot irons, has gone from 8.5c to 14c. Penwiper is now a devotee of random walk and spends board meetings doodling Boolean algebra on his notepad.

Pierpont's own strategy has been based on the theory that at some time in the next eighteen months there is going to be a sizeable run in the speculative miners. Your correspondent has therefore been picking up selected stocks and selling half the parcel once they have risen by about 20 per cent. So far Pierpont is showing modest profits and has accumulated a portfolio of residual half-parcels that will hopefully show large gains later. If the market turns sour, he will pull the ripcord and bale out of them all.

So there we are: five investors with five different theories, and although some of the theories are in total conflict we are all making money so none of us can be persuaded we're wrong. From which Pierpont concludes that a rising market makes any theory right just as a falling market makes any theory wrong.

Meanwhile, the mineral prospects of Blue Sky Mines are in a highly liquid condition, being under seven feet of northern Wet the last time anyone saw them.

PUTTING SOME BLUE SKY INTO THE ACCOUNTS

All Davidoff coronas being alight, the board meeting of Blue Sky was declared open. It was the June meeting at which we thrash out the contents of our annual report and as usual our figurehead chairman, Sir Mark Time, was absent. He needed little persuading that he should keep his lofty mind clear of the humdrum dogwork of preparing the accounts and stay an extra fortnight in Biarritz for the sake of his rheumatism. His presence at this meeting would have inhibited the free flow of ideas because there is always the danger, however, remote that he might emerge from his cataleptic trance long enough to work out what is happening.

Spender the accountant opened the meeting.

'First things first,' he said. 'Where are the auditors this year?'

'The Caribbean,' smiled young Penwiper. 'A fortnight ago we opened a two dollar subsidiary on Grand Cayman. As usual, we've sent the auditors to inspect it and of course they'll have to wait over in the Bahamas for a week each way to catch their connecting flights.'

'Did we get the signed certificate before they received the plane tickets?' asked Spender.

'Yes,' replied Penwiper. 'It's dated August.'

'Then we can start preparing the accounts,' said Spender. Lowering his voice, he asked: 'Where are the real books?'

Bottle the geologist pulled out a cobweb-encrusted plastic briefcase, unzipped it and removed the ledgers. He keeps them hidden down a disused mineshaft on one of our properties in the Simpson Desert.

Spender flicked over the pages. As usual Blue Sky had made a loss. It began the year with $200,000 left of its dwindling working capital. The directors managed to purloin $70,000 of this in overseas trips, lunches and cigars during the year and another $20,000 was spent on audit fees, including the Grand Cayman junket.

The remaining $100,000 of liquid assets is shown in the books as investments but actually it has all been lent to directors and will not be repaid under any circumstances.

'We have to show some administration expenses,' said Spender. 'So we'll claim $20,000 was spent on that. The rest of the year's expenditure, with a little judicious rewriting by Penwiper, will go down as exploration and development expenditure. We will write off 5 per cent of this sum against the profit and loss account and capitalise the rest by writing up the value of the prospects. This leaves us with a loss of just under $25,000. We can wipe that out by revaluing our stock of tungsten at Last Card by $30,000.'

'What stock of tungsten?' asked Penwiper.

'That big mound of rubble to the north of the old shaft,' explained Bottle. 'It contains a good tungsten grade, but it's metallurgically impossible to treat. So it's been there since '08 and will still be there next century. Under an accounting myth we're allowed to list it as an asset under the heading 'ore at grass'.'

Penwiper was struck by the concept. 'Tungsten prices have moved up since our last balance date,' he beamed. 'We could write it up further and declare a bigger profit.'

'Don't do that, son,' warned Pierpont. 'Or some ratbag shareholder might ask us to pay a dividend.'

In the Beginning, There Was Blue Sky . . .

Spender paled. 'I wish to reaffirm our basic principle,' he said in a deep, intense tone. 'that the proceeds of this company shall never be frittered away on benefits to the shareholders and I never wish to hear the expression . . .' (he almost choked on the word) '. . . dividend . . . within these walls again.'

He eased the tension by moving onto the next order of business. 'We've dressed up the accounts to give ourselves a marginal profit, but that's not going to move the shares,' Spender observed. 'Most of our shareholders don't read the accounts and I strongly suspect they can't even add up. What we need is exciting news from the field. Has there been any exploration lately?'

'Not by us,' said Bottle. 'But Desperate Drillers NL — you remember, the crowd who hold the claims on our western border — slipped across with an auger drill a few weeks ago and put down a few overnight holes.'

There was a stir of interest among the board. Such moonlight prospecting by a speculative company on a neighbour's property is by no means unknown in the Wild West. Even the mighty Ashton consortium was subject to such a raid a year ago, when a neighbouring company put at least one hole down on a kimberlite pipe and discovered indicator minerals. It was the talk of the stock exchange for weeks.

'It's flattering to know they think we're worth raiding,' said Spender. 'Do we happen to know what they found?'

'There's a clerk in their assay laboratory who owes me a bit of money,' said Bottle. 'He's a keen gambler.'

'I've been giving him a tip or two on the horses lately,' added Pierpont.

'Poor devil,' muttered Spender. 'What did he tell us?'

'They struck fair grades of tantalite,' said Bottle. 'I would guess from the sample numbers that the intersections were too widely dispersed to be economic, but that's only a guess.'

'Tantalite's very sexy at the moment,' mused Spender. 'Spot prices moved up beautifully this year.'

Penwiper had been shuffling through the month's share transfers. 'That explains why their nominee company has been picking up parcels of our scrip,' he said. 'I wonder when they're going to start leaking the news?'

'We'd better buy a few ourselves,' said Pierpont. 'And let's break out the Bolly.'

As we filled our glasses with the wine of the Marne, young Penwiper was already writing the chairman's review which would be signed by Sir Mark Time and included in the annual report.

'An active program of exploration continued during the year,' he wrote. 'Scout drilling revealed the presence of promising grades of tantalite to the west of the Last Card mine. Exploration is still in its preliminary stages on this prospect so any speculation about the value of the find would be premature. However, the price of tantalite during 1979 has been rising strongly . . .'

A CLEAR CASE OF A SALT

None of the directors yet having been sent to jail, we had a quorum and so the August board meeting of Blue Sky Mines No Liability was declared open. The board's deliberations were handicapped immensely by the presence of the chairman, that old dunderhead Sir Mark Time.

Even though he was in his usual state of near-catalepsy there was a danger that he might grasp what had been happening. And since his chief asset as a figurehead for Blue Sky is his complete ignorance of

In the Beginning, There Was Blue Sky . . .

the company's true state of affairs, the rest of the board had to dissemble.

We had tried, vainly, to lure him to Bermuda or the South of France for the week, but a touch of sinus had prevented him from flying. Pierpont had then suggested that Sir Mark should stay at his country property and nurse his condition, but the old drone insisted on coming to the city for the meeting. 'Can't let you chaps shoulder all the work,' he rumbled jovially. 'Wouldn't be fair, eh?'

So there he was, sitting at the head of the table like a statue carved out of cold porridge, while the rest of us wished he would somehow dematerialise.

Having pondered the agenda as though hypnotised for a good five minutes, Sir Mark finally broke the silence. 'I see the first item is the Starving Wombat scheelite prospect,' he said. 'Didn't we buy that from a prospector chappie about a month before the Newmarket?'

Bottle the geologist winced as though someone had probed an old wound. He had indeed acquired the Starving Wombat in the course of a very late night in Kalgoorlie's Palace Hotel. Old Harry Galena the prospector had poured so much Bollinger into Bottle that his hangover had been a topic of discussion for weeks afterwards.

From what the Blue Sky board could decipher of the agreement, written in Bearnaise sauce on a tablecloth, Blue Sky was committed to pay $500,000 for the claims. Fortunately Bottle's fiscal instincts had remained sound even while his higher intellect was drowning in premier cru and $475,000 of the vendor consideration was to be in Blue Sky shares at par.

Harry had induced Bottle into this disastrous purchase by producing an estimate that Starving Wombat had reserves of around a million tonnes of ore with a grade of 0.7 per cent scheelite. For the benefit of readers who are cloudy on metallurgy, scheelite is valuable because it is an ore of tungsten, which is used to make light filaments and to harden steel.

Seven-tenths of one per cent might not sound much to the layman, but it represents a good grade in scheelite. Peko-Wallsend works 0.75 per cent ore at King Island, and Tasminex NL mines a similar grade in Tasmania. Blue Sky promptly released this estimate to the stock exchanges and Blue Sky shares rose from 70 cents to a dollar.

'My memory must be getting hazy,' mumbled Sir Mark. 'I don't remember us making any statements about Starving Wombat since we released Galena's reserve estimate.'

There was an uneasy silence. Pierpont gazed at the ash on his cigar. Spender, the accountant, doodled a couple of logarithms on his pad. Bottle, from the expression on his face, was contemplating the homicide of Harry Galena. Young Penwiper, the secretary, said: 'I thought it better to make no further announcement until we had some firm news from the field, sir.'

To say this was paltering with the truth would be a gross understatement. Bottle, in a fit of alcoholic remorse after signing the agreement, had immediately conducted extensive tests of the claims. These had revealed Harry's reserve estimate to have been based solely on Bollinger. From some necessarily rough readings by fluorescent lamp on the drill cores, Harry had been out by at least a couple of decimal points and the best we could expect was 0.01 per cent. You could get as good a reading in your backyard, particularly if one of the children had dropped a transistor battery there.

If Blue Sky had a board of honourable directors the company would have announced the results of Bottle's tests to the stock exchanges straight away, downgrading the deposit. Naturally, we did no such thing.

'I take it we've been doing some work on the claims?' Sir Mark burbled hopefully.

'Oh, yes,' said Bottle. 'I've done quite a lot.'

That was true, anyhow. As soon as he realised how low the scheelite values were, Bottle had sacked the drill crew before they, too, found out. In a moment of inspiration, he even won some plaudits from the conservationists for saying the men had been dismissed for trespassing on an Aboriginal sacred site.

Then Bottle had rounded up all the used tungsten drill bits in the vicinity and had spent the next two days scraping the cutting edges off them with a rasp and salting the drill core samples with the filings. When he reckoned he had got the assay up to 1 per cent, he bagged the samples and sent them off to an assay laboratory.

'That's right,' Sir Mark exclaimed. 'We sent off samples for assay, didn't we? I must be getting absent-minded!'

In the Beginning, There Was Blue Sky . . .

What we hadn't known when we sent the samples off was that someone at the laboratory had been thinking along the same lines as Bottle. There had been a long delay in the assaying, during which time a nominee company had been buying heavily in Blue Sky stock. Blue Sky being a tightly held company (by the directors), this was akin to having a stranger suddenly appear with a fifth hand in a bridge game.

Then the long-delayed assay report arrived. The laboratory had cheerfully declared that Starving Wombat assayed 3.7 per cent scheelite. Bottle was horrified.

'You can't trust anyone these days,' he declared. 'I salted it to less than a third of that grade.'

Sir Mark was still moving along his ponderous thought process. 'Do we have the assay results?' he asked.

There was nothing for it. He had to be told.

Spender's face creaked into an accountant's smile. 'Here are the figures,' he said. 'You will find they average 3.7 per cent.'

'What!' exclaimed Sir Mark. 'That's great news! Great news! I'm amazed you chaps can stay so calm. I must telephone the exchange at once.'

He shuffled from the room, burbling 'Incredible! Incredible!' and you should hear the announcement on the floor any second now. Back in the boardroom, Spender broke his pencil and Pierpont helped himself to another Davidoff. It's a tight spot, but we think we see the way out.

The shares will go for a run, of course, and the nominee company will sell. So will the directors. Then Blue Sky will announce further drilling near an oddly shaped pile of stones, referring to them casually as being 'an unusual formation'.

This, together with Bottle's reference to a sacred site, should do the trick. Conservationists will call for a halt to exploration while anthropologists will proclaim the stones a sacred site.

The most casual check would reveal that the stones were dug up and pushed into their present shape by a bulldozer driver on roadworks in 1969, but the risk of any anthropologist checking facts opposed to his theories is remote.

As the battle rages, Sir Charles Court will ride to the rescue, declaring the exploitation of Starving Wombat to be vital to the national interest and at some point just before the whole issue reaches the United Nations, the directors of Blue Sky will sell the claims to Alan Bond or Holmes à Court or Ron Brierley or someone and tiptoe quietly away from the whole sordid affair.

SPRING – A TIME NOT TO GET SPRUNG

*'In the spring a livelier iris changes on the burnish'd dove;
In the spring a young man's fancy lightly turns to thoughts of love.'*

This description may well have fitted the young Tennyson in the Lincolnshire Wolds, but Pierpont has now reached crabbed age in the harsh brown land of Australia and finds that spring turns his fancy to money. In particular, spring turns your scribe's attention to balance sheets, which appear with the prevalence of locusts at this time of the year.

While preparing himself for this onslaught of pretty pictures, optimistic forecasts and black lies, it occurred to Pierpont that there may be a few benighted citizens who have not yet mastered the elements of balance sheet analysis.

So, in order that his readers may also be ready to cope with the accounts of their companies, your correspondent has drawn up the following explanatory article. The fee for this piece of tuition is a box of Bolivar coronas from each of you.

The accounts Pierpont has chosen for the exercise are those of Blue Sky Mines No Liability, in their simplified form. In their advanced form, after we have finished fiddling with Note One (principles used in compiling the accounts), they are quite unintelligible.

The classic way to distract shareholders from the accounts, of course, is to run pictures.

The annual report of Blue Sky, Pierpont regrets to say, does not run much to large, glossy, colour pictures. There are three reasons for this. First, the only large, glossy object which could be photographed is Pierpont's nose. Second, we cannot afford a photographer. Third, photographs of the board and our mining leases would hardly inspire confidence among potential buyers of the stock.

In the Beginning, There Was Blue Sky . . .

We have, however, borrowed a few photographs of geological specimens from the museum, which we will run in colour, together with some beautiful and highly complex maps of what Bottle imagines the rock strata is on our various prospects. If we ever get these maps back from the printer, we intend to enter them in the next contest for contemporary Australian abstract art. Last year the maps appeared upside down in the annual report, but fortunately no one noticed.

Now, if everyone is comfortably reclined, with a chilled bottle of the R.D.'69 Extra Brut at their elbow, Pierpont will take his readers through the books, starting with the profit and loss account.

BLUE SKY MINES NO LIABILITY
Profit and Loss Account

	$
Revenue (1)	100,000
Less: Expenses (2)	
Including: Interest $300,000; Directors' fees $100,000; Auditors' fees $20,000	820,000
Profit (loss)	(720,000)
Less future tax benefit	330,000
Net profit (loss)	(390,000)
Plus extraordinaries	3,000,000
Profit for year	2,610,000

1 Revenue: $100,000

Blue Sky managed to sell a few bags of tungsten ore from the Last Card scheelite mine during the year, but most of this figure is derived from interest on short-term funds.

Spender's brother-in-law is a bank manager who lends us money at low rates. If ever we don't need any for short periods, we lend it back to him at higher rates. We tip him off whenever Blue Sky shares are about to move and everyone is happy. As long as Blue Sky can stay out of receivership, the bank's head office will never know.

2 Expenses: $820,000

The actual mine working costs are very small, amounting to only $14,000 in 1978-79 (you'll see later how we reached this figure). The main cost was interest (Spender's brother-in-law had to charge us something). And while the auditors' fees only came to $20,000 as shown, we had to spend nearly another $100,000 on a round-the-world trip for them to investigate tungsten markets. Otherwise they'd never have signed these accounts.

Readers who have been tapping on their pocket calculators will have worked out that there are still several thousand dollars unaccounted for. That was almost entirely absorbed by directors' expenses, which are enormous. You may rest assured they will be even more enormous next financial year.

3 Future tax benefits: $330,000

For the benefit of the uninitiated, losses aren't losses any more. The fact that you've lost money means that you can write the loss off against future profits. Ergo, you have a future tax benefit. For a droll example of how this piece of high accounting lore works in practice, see the 1975 accounts of James Miller (Holdings) Ltd, in which a $2.1 million loss was reduced by $852,000 worth of future tax benefits. The company subsequently collapsed and Pierpont never heard of the receivers getting back a single cent for these benefits, which turned out to be truly intangible assets.

4 Extraordinaries: $3 million

This comprised a revaluation of the Last Card mine by $1 million, in view of rising tungsten prices and a revaluation of Blue Sky's head office by $2 million in view of rising rental values. The head office is admittedly only leasehold, but the valuer is Bottle's cousin. We give him tips on the shares, too, and are paying his expenses for six months' sabbatical leave in Gstaad this year.

5 Total profit: $2,610,000

Some companies would get carried away at this point and decide to declare a dividend. Blue Sky won't.

Passing lightly to the balance sheet, we start as usual with liabilities on the left.

In the Beginning, There Was Blue Sky . . .

BLUE SKY MINES NO LIABILITY

Liabilities				Assets		
June 1978 $		June 1979 $	June 1978 $			June 1979 $
1,000,000	Issued Capital[6]	1,000,000	2,000,000	Fixed Assets[10]		5,000,000
1,000,000	Reserves[7]	4,000,000	1,000,000	Current Assets[11]		3,000,000
2,000,000	Shareholders Funds	5,000,000	–	Intangibles[12]		430,000
750,000	Long Term Liabilities[8]	2,430,000	–	Investments[13]		1
250,000	Current Liabilities[9]	1,000,001	3,000,000	Total		8,430,001
3,000,000	Total	8,430,001				

1 Issued capital: $1 million

This consists of four million 25c shares, of which three-and-a-half million are held by the board through various nominees, aliases and deceased estates of great-aunts. The valuer and Spender's brother-in-law both sold out before taking their holidays.

2 Reserve: $4 million

Up by $3 million because of the revaluations. The other $1 million is historic and does not represent cash or assets of any kind. We hope that if we preserve it in the balance sheet for a few more years it will be classified by the National Trust.

3 Long-term liabilities: $2,430,000

If you add this and the current liabilities together, and compare the total with 1978, you will see that we had to borrow quite a lot of cash during the latest twelve months. No wonder Spender's brother-in-law is out of the country.

4 Current liabilities: $1 million

This is Blue Sky's expanded bank overdraft. The word 'current' normally implies liabilities which are due within twelve months. If you were allowed to look carefully at the long-term debts you would find that, although it was nominally arranged for twelve months and one day at the time it was taken out, it all falls due within the current calendar year. We argue that because it was originally taken out long term, it should stay under long term.

5 Fixed assets: $5 million

Note that the revaluation is $1 million larger than total shareholders' funds at the start of the financial year. This puts Blue Sky a notch ahead of Gollin, who in 1975 made a loss of $18 million, which would have almost exactly wiped out shareholders' funds if they had not had a revaluation of assets of $18 million. If it's good enough for Keith Gale, it's good enough for us.

6 Current assets: $3 million

On closer examination, this proves to consist entirely of written-up stock and trade creditors. There's not a skerrick of cash anywhere. The stock consists entirely of ore at grass. Our ore at grass looks like a weedy hill of rubble to a casual visitor, but rising tungsten prices have turned it into an appreciating asset and bank collateral. Whether we can ever sell it for book value is, of course, highly doubtful.

7 Intangibles: $430,000

Apart from the future tax benefit of $330,000, our main intangible is the pre-production expenses of $56,000. Behind this figure lies an interesting specimen of accounting lore.

During the year we spent $70,000 in various activities which could be somehow connected with the mine. As it is not yet in full production, we have put all this down as pre-production expenses. If we had written them off directly as costs, our profit would of course have dropped by $70,000 (or rather, our loss would have been increased by $70,000). But if we call them pre-production expenses they become intangible assets. We are writing them off at 20 per cent, which means we only took $14,000 directly into our expenses for 1978-79 and the other $56,000 remains on the books as an asset.

The final intangible item of $44,000 goodwill represents the value we have suddenly attached to the name of Blue Sky Mines, having been horrified to hear that one rapscallion WA prospector had actually registered a company of this name. We quantified the goodwill at $44,000 because this was the amount we needed to balance the two sides of the balance sheet.

In the Beginning, There Was Blue Sky . . .

8 Investments: $1

This represents Blue Sky's 50 per cent equity in a joint venture company called Krakatoa Properties, which is even shakier than the volcano of the same name. We don't even name Krakatoa in the annual report and shareholders would be given vague, confusing replies in the unlikely event that they ever asked about it. In fact, the company lost over $2 million last financial year, but as it isn't a subsidiary we haven't taken any of the loss into Blue Sky's results. Balance sheet analysts who have been wondering what happened to all the money we borrowed now know where it went, but the shareholders never will. Or not until we've all escaped to Argentina anyway.

It's the sort of investment that keeps your iris lively.

The Official History of Blue Sky Mines

TECHNICAL BRIEF 1

THE BLUE SKY POLICY ON ORE RESERVES

PRIVATE AND CONFIDENTIAL
Blue Sky Mines No Liability
Ore Reserves Policy

1. Geologists. Geologists employed by the company are divided into two categories: (a) Useful, and (b) Pictorial.

Those in category (a) are geologists who can cause a rise or fall as desired, in the share price. It therefore follows that they must only be paid in share options and never in cash. (Indeed, it is high policy that no Blue Sky Mines liability is ever incurred in cash.) Thus, any geologist holding a quarter of a million options exercisable at par of 25c has a strong incentive to report news that will send the share price to at least 25c. If the share price ever goes too high, say 50c, the board will short a quarter of a million shares on the geologist's behalf, giving him a fortnight to discover some disappointing news. Given the usual state of Blue Sky's prospects, this should not normally be difficult.

Geologists in category (b) are final year students, hired as a job lot from any nearby university on June 30. They are to be taken to the nearest unoccupied patch of scrub, loaned geologists' hammers and photographed in colour for the annual report. Their services are to be terminated on July 1.

2. Claim pegging. It is standing policy that Blue Sky only overpegs claims. This has the triple advantage of (a) making us appear to be in dispute over a 'hot' prospect; (b) giving us an outside chance of actually getting someone else's claim, if the warden has an attack of insanity; and (c) avoiding the necessity of having to spend money working the claim. If we pegged unencumbered ground as a claim, the shareholders might expect us to spend money exploring it.

3. Soil sampling, seismics, aeromagnetics, radiomagnetics. These forms of exploration are totally barred. They cost money and serve

In the Beginning, There Was Blue Sky . . .

no useful purpose. It is very hard to get the share market excited with some rock scratchings or a diagram of a seismic survey.

True, the Blue Sky accounts list an aircraft as an asset on the grounds that it conducts aeromagnetic surveys. In truth – as we all know – it is chartered out to other companies and never to be flown at the expense of Blue Sky. Except when the board and their wives go to Broome for holidays.

4. Percussion and diamond drilling. Drilling is a highly visible form of exploration and has the capacity to excite the sharemarket if used in the right environment. Prospects will therefore be drilled whenever we want to lift the share price.

The board is opposed to diamond drilling on the grounds of expense. Percussion drilling is cheaper and goes quite deep enough for our purposes. Few of the punters in the penny stocks know the difference between the two, and you can run a stock a long way on a percussion hole in any case. Remember that Poseidon went from $1 to $50 on the results of just one percussion hole.

If the board believes it will enhance the share price, we may from time to time announce that we are sinking diamond drillholes although in fact they are percussion. Only the contractor will ever know the difference and he will be long in the stock. If the truth is detected, we will simply say we made an accidental error.

Blue Sky will make its Panamanian subsidiary available for tax-free share trading by the contractor, and will pay his brokerage. This costs a little money, but is worth it to keep track of his buying and selling orders.

5. Announcements. Any drilling contractor working for Blue Sky must be instructed that his team is to stop drilling immediately if the rig strikes anything resembling ore. Then, if the assays return good grades, the company can announce that the orebody is open at depth. If we stop all other exploration as well, the orebody will also be open at width.

Strike length is of course purely notional, depending mainly upon how far the geologist can see on a clear day. It is Blue Sky policy that all strike lengths will be announced as between 500 and 900 metres. Strike lengths of more than one kilometre tend to lack credibility. The strike length will later be proved wrong, but this can always be excused on the grounds that the geologist misinterpreted the surface expressions. In the absence of any surface expressions, he will have misinterpreted the inferred geology.

6. Salting. The correct salting ratio is to be found in the expression $S = g \times 1.2\text{--}1.5$, where S is the salted sample and g the original grade of mineralisation. In brief, this means that staff are forbidden from enhancing grades by less than 20 per cent or more than 50 per cent.

It is a waste of time and effort to salt samples by less than 20 per cent. The upper limit of 50 per cent has been chosen as well within the bounds of assay or sampling error and will avoid geologists and directors becoming involved in tedious inquiries by the Corporate Affairs Commission or the Fraud Squad. Australia is littered with mines whose head grade is 30 per cent below their drilling assays, if you care to look back at them.

7. Assay sample delivery. It would he imprudent to commit our policy on this aspect to writing. However, we must all remember the episode which occurred in Victoria a few years ago when a vendor had farmed out a 50 per cent interest in a mineral prospect to a company. The company began drilling the prospect, but the results were disappointing.

Then the vendor, who was holding some shares in the company, intervened. 'I'll fix the problem,' he told the directors. 'Just let me deliver the cores.' They did, and the assays improved magically.

8. Abandonment. No prospect is ever abandoned. As long as a prospect stays on the books it can be assigned an asset value and promising discoveries can he made upon it. If the above policy is followed strictly, actual costs can be kept to a minimum, preferably zero.

Indeed, rather than explore a prospect, it is usually better to negotiate over it, which can be done for the price of a postage stamp. Thus if we send a letter to CRA offering it a stake in the last Card scheelite deposit, we can announce in the annual report that we are conducting negotiations with CRA. The fact that CRA will never reply to the letter is immaterial.

It must be confessed that this element of our policy is borrowed from the property development industry. If a developer has a building that nobody wants to buy, he says he has 'expressions of interest'. If you stop three pedestrians in Collins Street, ask them

In the Beginning, There Was Blue Sky . . .

if they would like to own BHP House and they say 'yes', you have three expressions of interest.

9. Reserves. The tonnage of Blue Sky's ore reserves always rises. However, to stop them reaching an incredible size, this is best achieved by adjusting the figure for the previous year.

Thus in 1988, we announced that reserves had risen from 80,000 tonnes to 100,000 tonnes. Then in 1989 we announced that reserves had risen from 85,000 tonnes to 105,000 tonnes.

This procedure is almost perfectly safe because nobody, but nobody, ever checks back on the figures in the last annual report. In the event that some busybody does notice that last year's figure has suddenly shrunk, we tell them that we have reassessed the cut-off grade, a figure which we never publish anyway.

Blue Sky's reserves are never stated as being proven, probable, inferred or any other term capable of technical definition. If anyone asks, say they are implied (usually by consulting an astrologer).

10. Grade. All Blue Sky deposits must have a grade just bordering on viability. If the grade is too low, the punters will write off the deposit. If it is too high, they will expect us to mine it. The current policy of the board is that any gold deposit we discover will have a grade of 1.36 grams per tonne.

This figure, however, was set some time ago and is becoming dangerously close to viability, so may soon have to be revised. Also, we may have to reduce the figure if the gold price rises. As we are never going to mine the deposit, there is no danger of the figure being proved wrong.

OVERVIEW. This policy is to be interpreted in the light of Blue Sky's overall policy that this company will NEVER, under any circumstances, actually mine anything. Mining minerals is dirty, hazardous expensive and frequently unprofitable.

Blue Sky's objective is to mine the shareholders, an occupation which in Australia has historically proved to be highly profitable and almost riskless.

N.B. This report is printed on rice paper. Any director arrested by the CAC while in possession of this document should eat it immediately.

PERTH RESEARCH ANALYST
EXCITED SHAREBROKER
BOTTLE, THE GEOLOGIST
ASSAYER DISCOVERS TUNGSTEN IN ORE
WATER TABLE
CRIB
ORE BEING SALTED WITH OLD TRANSISTOR BATTERIES
WORKFORCE

The LAST CARD
TUNGSTEN MINE
from the Annual Report of Blue Sky Mines
TELEPHONE
COSTEAN
DISCOVERY HOLE
WHICH INTERSECTED
HIGH-GRADE ZONE
AND FINISHED
IN ORE
HIGH-GRADE
ZONE
RABBIT
WARREN
ORE

INTO THE 1980s

Gold ran to its historic peak of $US800 an ounce in January 1980. But there were still only a few working gold mines in Australia, so Blue Sky was slow to announce that it had struck gold. We don't like to be too conspicuous.

The share market was jagged. It slumped in early 1981, ran at the finish of that year, then slumped again in 1982.

Malcolm Fraser gave us a short, sharp recession in 1982-83 and then wondered why the electorate threw him out of office.

The Falklands War was started by Argentina in April 1982 and finished by the British in June.

MacArthur River was spoken of as a great future mine. The all ordinaries had hit 760 in late 1980 but was back below 500 in 1982.

The job of policing the corporate sector was taken over by the National Companies and Securities Commission, who were sternly vigilant.

IN SEARCH OF A SMALL, CREDIBLE LOSS

It might as well be confessed straight away that the directors of Blue Sky Mines were a trifle below par at their board meeting last week.

The chairman, that old imbecile Sir Mark Time, is ponderous even when at his best. The first cold snap of winter appears to have sent his faculties into hibernation, which means that instead of being in a semi-coma at board meetings, he is fully cataleptic.

Even so, he was in better form than Pierpont and Spender the accountant, who had spent the previous evening at the Croesus Club celebrating their profits on the bank takeovers. The old club was pretty well awash with Bollinger all night, and events had taken their toll. Spender, who had spent the night proposing a series of toasts to his hero, Ivar Kreuger, was now clutching his ashen brow and staring sightlessly at his notepad. Pierpont, who had polished off a decanter – or it may have been two – of Grandfather port as a chaser, was in an advanced state of decay, feeling much as though he had spent the night in a Pioneer concrete truck.

In any normal gathering your correspondent would have been voted Corpse of the Day, but on this occasion he was eclipsed by Bottle the geologist. Bottle had just returned from a field trip to Kalgoorlie, where he had spent a solid week pegging claims in the corner bar of the Palace. He had been consuming Hannas by day to ward off the heat and Bundaberg OP by night to protect him from the cold. The air hostess on the return flight genuinely believed he should have been travelling on a stretcher. He had not slept on the Redeye and was now slumped bloodshot in his chair looking like a sculpture carved hurriedly from guano.

To make it unanimous, Penwiper, our poor but dishonest secretary, was also under the weather. He is currently contending with three mortgages, four overdue margin calls on gold futures and Mrs Penwiper, and Pierpont feels he is fighting out of his division. Mrs Penwiper, a young and ambitious harridan, would disembowel the boy if she knew he has been losing in the futures market, and he has been keeping her at bay by painting a rosy and inaccurate picture of his current finances and immediate prospects. She has seized upon this as an excuse to buy a new wardrobe on Bankcard, which means that

The Official History of Blue Sky Mines

Penwiper's most imminent prospect is bankruptcy — and judging from the glint in his eye at night when he goes home to Mrs Penwiper, perhaps a homicide charge as well. He has taken to Teachers to ease the strain and was hung over again as the board met.

We all had five minutes' rest as Sir Mark studied the agenda. Finally he said: 'There's only one item on this. It says: "Determine year's profit." What does that mean?'

The old drone had a point, if only he'd realised it. There is a theory, sometimes encountered in the more unworldly business administration courses, that a company's profit is determined by accountants adding up the year's revenue and then subtracting the expenses. This, of course, is pure theory and barely countenanced even in correspondence courses. In the real world, as everybody knows, the directors first choose a figure for their profit (or sometimes loss) for the twelve months and then adopt a set of accounting techniques which will enable them to reach their desired number.

On this issue, Blue Sky adheres to the mainstream of Australian business practice. The most acceptable result for Blue Sky's image would be a small loss. If we declared a profit, some moronic shareholder might ask for a dividend. More importantly, none of the institutions would believe us, thereby impairing our future hopes for loans or share placements. A large loss would also shock these important people, so obviously we have to declare a small, credible loss.

Blue Sky started the latest year in remarkably liquid condition. Thanks to share market euphoria, Blue Sky's shares became as overpriced as everyone else's (partly due to a few creative announcements by the board) and we managed to raise just over $1 million through a rights issue and two placements. Since then we have spent $400,000 in exploration expenditure and administrative overheads, which, together with a few other items, means the loss for the year could be regarded as $430,000. Could be, that is, if you're a business administration student.

The problem is the $400,000 exploration expenditure.

As several hundred kangaroos and bandicoots could testify, none of this money has been expended on Blue Sky's only mining prospect, the Last Card scheelite deposit. What the sum represents is exploration of claims at the Palace by Bottle, exploration of rumours at the Croesus Club by Pierpont and exploration by Spender of techniques by which these sums could be included in the exploration expenditure account. There was also a gold lamé evening gown for Mrs Penwiper, entered under the heading of 'geophysical surveys'.

'Looks like we've lost $430,000,' frowned Sir Mark, studying the figures.

'Not really,' replied Spender, polishing his rimless spectacles. 'You mustn't think of exploration expenditure as money lost. It is an investment in the Last Card deposit. By spending this money on the deposit we have increased our knowledge of it and enhanced its value, so we will capitalise the expenditure by adding it on to the previous value of Last Card.'

'But aren't exploration companies supposed to write off exploration expenditure as it's incurred?' asked Sir Mark.

'Not if the costs are expected to be recouped,' said Spender.

'I don't know if I ever expect to see a penny out of Last Card,' moaned Sir Mark. 'We seem to have been exploring it forever. Furthermore, I was reading the annual report by Buka Minerals NL the other day and I noticed they write off all their expenditure every year. And here's another from Magnet Metals Ltd, who also write off all their exploration as it's incurred.'

'Traitors,' muttered Spender, but Pierpont felt the matter was too urgent for recriminations. 'I think you'll find the 1980 report of Woodside Petroleum reassuring,' your correspondent told Sir Mark. 'You will see from note 14 that they have written off no exploration costs, even though they relinquished a substantial proportion of their exploration permits. I understand they just capitalise the lot on the grounds that the expense will be recovered through future sales.'

'What did the auditors say?' asked Sir Mark.

'Ernst & Whinney have given Woodside an unqualified report,' replied Pierpont. 'And you'll be interested to know that Buka are appointing Ernst & Whinney as auditors for 1981.'

'Perhaps we should have them too,' suggested Sir Mark. 'Is Woodside a respectable company?'

Pierpont played his trump. 'The major shareholders are Shell and BHP,' your correspondent said.

'BHP!' Sir Mark exclaimed. 'It must be all right then.'

So he signed the accounts, capitalising the $400,000 as an asset and leaving our loss at $30,000. Small, but credible.

Bottle's eyes flickered. 'I'll pay three hundred dollarsh each for sheventeen diamond claimsh,' he slurred. 'Mush be a good addresh . . .'

'Relax, old boy,' said Pierpont. 'You're back in civilisation now. What say we go around to the club for an aperitif, eh?'

DANCING THE THREE-STEP CONTRA

All directors being present — and as sentient as they were likely to get — the board meeting of Blue Sky Mines was declared open.

Sir Mark Time was as alert as usual, which is to say that he was near-moribund. If Blue Sky ever falls on hard times, we may invite an art gallery director to one of our meetings and sell off Sir Mark as a statue.

For fully the first five minutes of the meeting, nothing happened. Sir Mark sat staring blankly at the agenda for so long that Pierpont seriously began wondering whether he may have forgotten how to read. Your correspondent and the other directors occupied themselves by piercing their Carl Upmanns, lighting up and contemplating infinity. The only constructive activity was being undertaken by our young secretary Penwiper, an industrious lad, who was busily forging the minutes in advance.

At long last Sir Mark spoke. 'I see the first item is a proposal to buy 90 per cent of the Starving Wombat field from a Macao company called Dim Sim Minerals for $2 million,' he said. 'I'm afraid I haven't been following our affairs too closely of late, so I'm a little unfamiliar with this one. Is . . . er . . . is it a good prospect?'

Bottle, as the company geologist, replied at length, talking about chrome diopside, magnesium ilmenite, pyrope garnet, pipes, bort, alluvium, resistivity surveys and geochemical prospecting. Pierpont paid no attention to this technological smokescreen because he knew the real story. Starving Wombat was originally a scheelite prospect and once was even owned by Blue Sky (which Sir Mark had conveniently forgotten) but its area did include a barren kimberlite pipe. If anyone ever checks the records they will find it was explored briefly by a South African major a decade ago and relinquished. The claim

Into the 1980s

was taken up by Dim Sim Minerals a few months back and, after a short period of apparent activity, they announced the discovery of five small but promising diamonds.

This was a pure case of salting. The diamonds were planted in sample bags from the pipe, before being assayed. Pierpont knows, because he, Spender and Bottle are the owners of Dim Sim Minerals, via a Jersey trust, a Port Vila nominee and a numbered Zug account.

'I think I remember this mine now,' recalled Sir Mark, becoming excited. 'Doesn't another public company own the other 10 per cent?'

Correct. The other 10 per cent is held by Desperate Drillers No Liability, a speculative company whose affairs make Blue Sky appear a pillar of rectitude. At the same time that the diamond discovery was announced, Desperate Drillers had bought its 10 per cent stake in Starving Wombat for $300,000.

Pierpont could almost hear the cogs grinding as Sir Mark wrestled with the arithmetic. Desperate Drillers had paid $300,000 for 10 per cent. Add a nought and that made it ... er ... probably $3 million for the value of the whole prospect, near as dammit. Now Blue Sky was being offered 90 per cent for $2 million.

The Official History of Blue Sky Mines

'It's a bargain,' beamed Sir Mark. 'How did you chaps manage it?'

'We beat the vendors down a bit,' Spender smiled modestly.

A thought strayed into what, for want of a better word, must be called Sir Mark's mind.

'How are we going to pay for it?' he asked. 'Blue Sky hasn't got $2 million, as I recall.'

'That's item number two on the agenda,' piped Penwiper. 'A premium issue to shareholders to finance our priceless acquisition.'

'Don't rush me, boy,' huffed Sir Mark. 'I haven't read that far yet.'

Silence reigned once more as Sir Mark studied the proposal. Blue Sky is issuing an attractive package of fully paid shares, part paid shares, three-year options, five-year options, cumulative participating unsecured convertible notes and luncheon vouchers, raising $2.5 million in a mixture that would confuse Jim Wolfensohn. The key elements are the fully paid shares and the options, which are being issued to shareholders at little over half their current market prices. A broking firm has underwritten the issue. What the broking firm is really doing, of course, is propping the shares on market so that all the shareholders will take up their entitlements. Then the firm will pick up its fees and leave the market to destiny.

Sir Mark, having tried to read the terms of the issue four times without ever reaching the halfway mark, finally threw in the sponge.

'It seems a bit complicated,' he said. 'But I'm sure you chaps know what you're doing. Is there anything else on the agenda?'

'Item three,' said Penwiper. 'It follows item two.'

We all lit fresh Upmanns as Sir Mark studied the third proposal, which was to invest $300,000 to purchase 10 per cent of a broadacres real estate development from Desperate Drillers. Our nonchalance masked a slight apprehension because there was always a chance that Sir Mark might ask some technical question, such as where the land was. None of us had the foggiest notion. Knowing Desperate Drillers, it was most probably below the high tide mark somewhere.

But this was the contra. Desperate Drillers had paid $300,000 for 10 per cent of Dim Sim's lease, thereby establishing its total value as $3 million. Now we had to do the same for their patch of swampland. As Desperate Drillers had no money, it could not send a cheque to Dim Sim until it had received a cheque for the same amount from Blue Sky.

Spender was carrying on a long monologue about the land boom in Australia and Sir Mark, impatient for lunch, said: 'Yes, well I don't see how we can go wrong' – and was promptly ushered out of the door by Pierpont for aperitifs at the Croesus Club while Penwiper declared the meeting over.

All very satisfactory. The shareholders will put $2.5 million into Blue Sky. On a valuation established by Desperate Drillers – with whom we have no connection through shareholdings or directorships – Blue Sky will pay Dim Sim $2 million for 90 per cent of Starving Wombat. Another $300,000 of the $2.5 million will be collected by Dim Sim through Desperate Drillers. Pierpont, Spender and Bottle will have milked, through an elaborate screen of foreign companies, $2.3 million out of Blue Sky's shareholders.

Desperate Drillers do not mind being a party to the deal, because it has cost them nothing and they have established a valuation on their real estate project, which is going to be used for similar purposes.

The only regrettable aspect of the scheme is that Blue Sky will still retain $200,000 of the $2.5 million.

But – with Pierpont, Spender and Bottle as directors – not for long.

THE YEAR OF THE DRAGON

Shuffling across the street, half crippled by gout, Pierpont noticed a familiar cadaverous figure at the corner where the old blind beggar stands.

It was Leo Liability the stockbroker, whose portfolio of penny dreadful mining stocks is now looking like the Hindenburg on the day after. He was standing suspiciously close to the beggar and Pierpont has the strong feeling that if your correspondent had not come along the blind man might have been short a few cents from his tin cup.

'Leo, you low hound,' cried Pierpont. 'How's the market?'

'Down six points today,' replied Leo.

'The last stock you sold me has only got six points left in it,' snarled Pierpont. 'So I presume it's been wiped out.'

Your correspondent stamped his foot in annoyance, sending a bolt of white-hot pain shooting from ankle to cranium. When the mists of agony cleared, Leo had disappeared and so had the blind man's cup and seeing-eye dog.

'It could be worse,' Pierpont consoled the blind chap. 'You could be a client of his.'

Pierpont tottered along gingerly to the offices of Blue Sky Mines No Liability, where the monthly board meeting was about to begin.

As he limped into the boardroom, Pierpont noticed that you could have cut the atmosphere with a knife. Of course you can often cut the Blue Sky boardroom atmosphere with a knife, especially when Pierpont and Spender the accountant and Bottle the geologist have been smoking their Medallion coronas, but what Pierpont means is that the atmosphere was tense.

Apart from Bottle and Spender, those present were young Penwiper, and our chairman, Sir Mark Time. Sir Mark was ashen.

'The most dreadful thing has happened,' Sir Mark croaked. 'We've been queried by the NCSC.'

Pierpont sat down and reached for the cigar box, concerned but far from distraught. On a Bad News Scale where buying a losing Lotto ticket rates one and being bankrupted rates 10, a query from the National Companies and Securities Commission comes in at about three and a quarter. Indeed, it may not rate on the Bad News Scale at all, because Pierpont knows most of the people who are in regular receipt of NCSC queries and most of them are millionaires.

Perhaps they send a cheque out with each query. Pierpont asked Sir Mark whether this was so.

'No, they didn't send a cheque,' he snorted testily. 'They sent a letter asking what happened to the money we raised in our latest call.'

Pierpont drew thoughtfully on his Medallion. He was none too surprised by the query. Having decided that the speculative game is over for the moment, we decided to clean out the holders of the contributing shares issued last year with a hefty call. So we put a 15c call on at a time when the shares were standing at 20c. Theoretically we stood to raise $27 million for the company, but in practice the shares nose-dived to five cents which meant that the 15c call would be paid only by shareholders who were mentally deficient.

Into the 1980s

It was encouraging to learn that there are still a few of these around. We received $500,000 in call money from small holders. Obviously, we are going to have to put a bigger call on in a few months to shake these head cases out. The directors, of course, did not pay the call. We have better things to do with our money than to invest it in shaky ventures such as Blue Sky. The original cost of these shares was only a few cents and has been covered many times over by trading gains, so we can afford the sacrifice.

'What happened to that half million we raised?' asked Sir Mark. 'If we can't explain it, I shan't be able to look any of the chaps at the club in the eye again.'

He was referring to the Croesus Club, and Pierpont is dashed if he knows why anyone would want to go around looking at the eyes of the members there. Pierpont has looked at hundreds and they are all either bloodshot or glassy. You'd be better off looking at the wallpaper.

Young Penwiper piped up. 'That was our diversification, Sir Mark. If you remember, the overseas investment rules had just been relaxed at the time, so we took the opportunity to buy a venture capital company in California.'

'That's right,' recalled Sir Mark, his face clearing. 'We can explain this easily. Bought it from a company called Creative Investments Corporation in San Diego. Run by a couple of promising young accountants.'

Creative and promising they certainly were. Creative Investments was set up overnight by Spender, Bottle and Pierpont with a couple of off-duty surfies hired as directors for the occasion. The instant the deal was negotiated the surfies on-loaned the $500,000 to a Hong Kong company called Dragon's Breath Enterprises and disappeared. Where they went, Pierpont does not know, but the Mexican border was only half a gallon of petrol away. They were paid $5,000 for their trouble and are supposed to drop a pre-printed balance sheet into the mail in twelve months' time.

Tracing the ownership of Dragon's Breath Enterprises is harder than finding the Loch Ness monster. All the shares are held by a Swiss bank nominee company, and any investigator who has the time and expense account to trace the beneficial ownership will find it is a trust in Grand Cayman, which is in turn managed by a company in

Liechtenstein, whose key directors and shareholders are residents of the Bahamas. Regular readers do not need to be told that the real beneficial owners of Dragon's Breath are Pierpont, Bottle and Spender, but it would take a quarter of the NCSC's budget to prove this in court.

Dragon's Breath, you may recall, recently spent $500,000 as a down payment on tungsten claims in Western Australia. These claims, which adjoin Blue Sky's Last Card scheelite prospect, were previously held by Bottle, Spender and Pierpont. The full price of the claims was $2 million, which means Dragon's Breath must pay another $15 million within the next year. Pierpont can tell you now that it will default.

Which brings us to the bottom line. Innocent small shareholders have put $500,000 into Blue Sky Mines. Blue Sky invested the money in a San Diego company which might as well be non-existent. Pierpont, Spender and Bottle have made a capital profit by selling for $500,000 mining claims which cost them $10,000, and they will get the claims back anyway when Dragon's Breath defaults. Blue Sky benefits because a value of $2 million has been placed on neighbouring claims by a wily Celestial company, which means it can write up the value of Last Card to $2 million also, improving its net asset backing.

It would be nice if we could have helped Blue Sky's profit and loss account as well, but God Almighty couldn't do much with that mess. Which means that everyone's a winner except the shareholders, but they must have a death wish or they wouldn't have bought Blue Sky shares in the first place.

AN IMPRESSIONIST ANNUAL REPORT

All directors of Blue Sky Mines being present (none having yet had to flee to Costa Rica) the monthly board meeting was declared open.

In the chair as usual sat old Sir Mark Time. One could describe him as a man with an ice-cold brain, because as far as Pierpont can ascertain the space between his ears is filled by nothing except frozen gelatine. No thought has ever penetrated his cranium, which is just as well because otherwise he might occasionally wonder what the rest of the board are doing.

Into the 1980s

This being the annual report meeting, Spender was doodling a few figures on a notepad and Bottle was examining a few rocks he had bought in the Argent Hotel at Mount Isa to provide a pretty picture for our 1981 cover. Young Penwiper, our poor but dishonest secretary, could see there would be little work for him at this meeting so he was filling in time by writing up the 1982 minutes in advance, including the announcement of an exciting scheelite strike next April.

Pierpont was immersed in a document entitled *The Annual Report Book: A step by step management system for your annual report*. At first glance, Pierpont had almost consigned it to the universal filing unit, but had stayed his hand because he had long felt that Blue Sky's annual report needed a little gingering up.

The numbers at the back of the report present few problems because Blue Sky has developed financial planning to a fine art. Blue Sky declared a small loss last year, and Pierpont can tell you it will be the same again this year. In 1983 we intend to give the market a pleasant surprise by announcing a small profit, but in 1984 we'll be back into a small loss again. Never a large loss, because that worries lenders and never a big profit because some fool shareholder might ask for a dividend.

Our balance sheet is well planned too. Many dollars will march through the exploration account but very little of this will represent mine development. Shareholders' funds will expand in booms as we raise capital from shareholders and will shrink in recessions as we reduce capital and announce heavy calls to drive shareholders out again. Spender's major task will be to apply generally accepted accounting principles to disguise the fact that capital subscriptions by shareholders are being redirected to a network of private companies controlled by the board.

We are therefore a highly predictable company for the next five years unless Spender runs out of generally accepted accounting principles (highly unlikely) or Blue Sky's affairs are disrupted by a major Corporate Affairs Commission investigation (6/4 on according to the current quotation from the Croesus Club bookmaker).

The place where we always have trouble is the chairman's report. Sir Mark being a pure figurehead, we like to let him say a few words about the company on the opening page each year. However, the way Blue Sky operates, the less said about its affairs the better. The more words Sir Mark puts on paper in ignorance, the more likely he is to stray from the company's true state of affairs. Lest your correspondent give the wrong impression, let him hasten to add that several words in Blue Sky's last annual report were perfectly true, notably 'a', 'the' and the address of the registered office.

So now you know why Pierpont was reading *The Annual Report Book*, starting at the page entitled 'The Quest for Corporate Recognition'.

The first paragraph to catch Pierpont's eye read: 'The passing of time has dimmed the origin of annual reports as a statutory reporting vehicle for shareholders. Within the financial arena, they have become more and more a vehicle for influencing existing and potential stakeholders, whether they be sources of finance, employees, community interest groups or others. In reality, the annual report is a composite corporate advertisement which tells many people what a company does and gives an impression of how well it does it.'

Pierpont almost cried 'Eureka!', as Archimedes did on discovering gin in his bathtub. The document appeared to be describing exactly the sort of annual report Blue Sky was seeking.

Mind you, Blue Sky does not always quest for corporate recognition. On several occasions when making announcements about exploration results we would have preferred to have done so incognito. Indeed, Penwiper once considered requesting to the stock exchange that the shares be quoted anonymously.

But the rest of the remarks apply exactly to Blue Sky. We are all in favour of dimming the statutory reporting side of the annual report, and the dimmer the better. We would much prefer to influence stakeholders and financiers, present the report as a composite corporate advertisement and just give an impression of what we've been doing.

WHAT BEARS DO IN HIBERNATION

The chairman having ceremonially drawn the stopper from the port decanter, the board meeting of Blue Sky Mines No Liability was declared open.

Into the 1980s

The grand old company has been none too active lately, a characteristic it shares with the board. We had not seen each other for so long we needed introductions.

What do directors of speculative companies do during bear markets? It's rather like asking what Collingwood supporters do during the cricket season or what soldiers do when peace breaks out.

In the case of Blue Sky Mines, the directors have sensibly contracted the company's activities so that it has been running purely at administrative costs for the past six months. A shareholder at the annual meeting (postponed) last year described us coarsely as management fee bludgers and was expelled from the proceedings.

In fact, Blue Sky has not held a directors' meeting since October and even the gnarled consciences of the board were stirred by the thought that we should make some token gesture of attending to the shareholders' interests, so we got together last Friday.

Corporeally, the chair was occupied by Sir Mark Time. Pierpont uses the word 'corporeally' because spiritually Sir Mark was in the third bowge of Dante's Inferno. The old fool buys shares in only one company, which is BHP, and recently his sufferings have been intense. In Sir Mark's mind, the idea that BHP is A Good Company may be likened to a fly caught in a drop of glue on the Holden production line. It emerges into daylight only after taking the full buffeting that the stock market can inflict.

The buffeting has been considerable lately because in a bear market the shares in good companies fare nearly as badly as those of poor ones. So far in 1982, BHP has gone from a high of $10.55 to as low as $7. Worse, when the company announced a rights issue at $9, Sir Mark enlarged his holding so he could take up more stock. The shares are now down to $7.46 and the expression on Sir Mark's face is distressing to behold. He looks like a sheep that has just stepped into a dingo trap.

The rest of the Blue Sky board at Friday's meeting were scarcely more constructive. Spender was nursing an acute hangover and Pierpont was bemused by the flood of congratulatory mail (two letters) marking his tenth anniversary as a scribe. Young Penwiper was being more useful. He was forging the minutes of all the meetings we should have held since Christmas to comply with the Companies Act. He's a thoughtful lad, and his fitful efforts to keep the directors out of jail are greatly appreciated. We would pay him a salary if Blue Sky had any money.

In bull markets, Blue Sky's strategy is to make optimistic statements about exploration we are going to commit and claims we are going to buy in order to enhance the company's share price. In bear markets we simply cease activity. There is no point in making optimistic statements in bad times, so we save them for better times.

Then a courier arrived with a bottle of Dom Perignon, sent to Pierpont by an admirer. Tears welled in Pierpont's rheumy old eyes when he saw from the accompanying letter that it had been sent by his favourite entrepreneur, Peter Briggs.

Spender, still clutching his brow to contain a hangover that looked as though it must have measured about force six on the Richter scale, said: 'Pass it along. I need a hair of the dog.'

'No fear,' said Pierpont, then paused. 'On second thoughts, you can have the first glass.'

'I'll take it,' croaked Spender. 'I've nothing to lose.'

Pierpont sympathised. As Blue Sky has been in a state of suspended animation since well before Christmas, Spender has had nothing to do except infest the bar of the Croesus Club, where he has been inflicting extensive damage on his liver. But such is the magic of Dom that after a glass he managed some semblance of life again.

'Let's take this meeting in hand,' he cried.

So then and there we mapped out Blue Sky's strategy for the next six months. The first action will be a one-for-one rights issue to shareholders at the fully paid value of 50c a share. As the old company's stock has fallen from a dizzy $1.50 in 1980 to 3c recently, the response to this will be overwhelmingly negative. We will then rig a forfeited share auction at which the new issue will be flogged to our own nominee companies at a discount. The next step will be to ram a motion through an extraordinary meeting approving a capital reduction and we will have squeezed the proportion of Blue Sky held by outside shareholders down from the present 53 per cent to less than a quarter.

Then, equipped with a nice, tight capital structure, we will acquire the cheapest group of claims we can find in the most fashionable area and mineral at the time, and Blue Sky will be all set for its next market run.

Quite simple, really. A glimmer of hope flickered even in Sir Mark's eyes.

'Sounds like good planning,' he said. 'Perhaps BHP should do something like this.'

Well, we're available to advise them. For a management fee, of course.

GETTING YOUR PRIORITIES RIGHT

As June dawns, it is not a moment too early to begin planning how to falsify this year's accounts. From a fast scan around Australia's public listed companies, Pierpont can see that his peers have very little need of tuition in this branch of the arts. However, on the off-chance that a few benighted company secretaries still need a checklist, Pierpont is prepared to offer his advisory services for the usual fee (half a dozen jewelled snuffboxes at Christmas).

The best guide your correspondent can give is from the last board meeting of Blue Sky Mines No Liability, where the annual report was debated. The order of the agenda ran as follows:

1. Date of mailing
2. Location of annual meeting
3. Colour of paper
4. Auditors' travel arrangements
5. Size of loss
6. Selection of photos and artwork
7. Valuation of liabilities
8. Note one
9. Valuation of assets
10. Visa check
11. Miscellaneous (balance sheet, profit-and-loss account, tax, depreciation, etc).

To be objective, Pierpont must admit that some recognised authorities differ from your correspondent. Mandamus and Catfish (Malpractice Press, 1957) claim that solicitors' fees should be the third item on the agenda and that the remainder of the proceedings should be conducted in the Bahamas, while Horatio Cufflink (*The Ethical Basis of Arson*, 1967) believes the first order of business should be setting fire to the share register.

But these, of course, are mere quibbles.

The mainstream of Australian corporate thought is based on the premise that both flight and fire are an evasion of directors' responsibilities and that shareholders should be deluded in a manly, straightforward fashion.

This brings us to point one of Pierpont's agenda – the date of mailing of the annual report. Other aspects of the Blue Sky accounts may be put together in a light-hearted, slapdash fashion (contingent liabilities and the directors' CVs come to mind) but the date of mailing is calculated with exquisite care.

This year the annual reports of Blue Sky will be mailed at Footscray at 5 p.m. on Friday, 21 October. This date is calculated by first working out the date of the annual meeting, which will be at 9 a.m. on 5 November. This puts Blue Sky just within the fourteen-day minimum period which the law says should occur between mailing of the annual report and the holding of the annual meeting.

Proxies must be lodged at least 48 hours before the annual meeting, that is at 9 a.m. on Wednesday, 3 November. As everyone knows, no post office in Australia delivers mail before 9 a.m., so this means the only effective proxies will be those delivered on Tuesday, 2 November. Tuesday, 2 November, is Melbourne Cup Day, so we are really talking about those proxies which reach the registered office (at Mooroopna) by Monday, November 1.

The way the postal system works, these letters will have to reach the GPO in Elizabeth Street by some time on Thursday, 27 October.

As the annual reports were not mailed until late on Friday, 21 October, the earliest they will reach shareholders is by the morning mail of Tuesday, 25 October. That is, if the shareholders live within the Melbourne metropolitan area.

And even then they will effectively have only two days to lodge their proxies.

Actually, Australia Post has been showing ominous signs of efficiency lately, and the Blue Sky board is a trifle worried. If more than a dozen shareholders manage to lodge proxies in time this year, we intend to shift the company's head office to Darwin.

The second and third items on the agenda warranted no discussion. The annual meeting will be held at Mooroopna again and the annual report will be printed in a small, spidery, blue type on dark blue paper. This is difficult to read and quite impossible to photocopy.

The fourth item took longer, but eventually the fine old (1979) audit firm of Halt and Lame settled for two weeks in Acapulco investigating a $2 subsidiary we set up there solely for that purpose. This being settled, Halt and Lame signed the annual report as being true and fair.

Next we had to decide on the size of the loss. There is no question of Blue Sky making a profit because of the danger, however remote, that some shareholders might begin expecting us to pay a dividend. Nor do we want a large loss, because that attracts headlines. Eventually we decided to lose about $80,000 for the year.

Some companies still tot up their assets and liabilities before discovering whether they have made a profit or loss for the year. This is unscientific.

It is for the same reason that Blue Sky assesses its liabilities before its assets.

Liabilities are a set, unalterable figure. Having determined the size of Blue Sky's loss and the total of its liabilities (mostly hapless trade creditors because no bank in its right mind would lend us money), it is then a simple matter to determine how large Blue Sky's assets should be to cover the liabilities. We then decide on how assets should be revalued to reach this figure and write the relevant accounting principles into note one.

The principles of both valuation and accounting being infinitely flexible, this presents no large problem.

Which is just as well, because after ensuring that our visas to Ecuador are still valid, we hand the rest of the tedious paperwork over to the company secretary and retire for a well-earned lunch at the Croesus Club.

UNDER ANALYSIS

Pierpont was in his study splitting his personal shareholdings to take maximum advantage of the dividend rebates provided in the 1982 budget. To aid him in this undertaking, your correspondent had recruited Mrs Pierpont, who rarely ventures into the den for fear of asphyxiating in the Monte Cristo smoke.

'We'll start by splitting the ANZ stock,' muttered Pierpont. 'A thousand in dividends for me, a thousand for you, all tax free. Now who else do we have in the family?'

Mrs Pierpont looked up from her knitting (she's producing balaclavas for the lads garrisoning the Falklands) and said: 'What about the children?'

'Can't stand any of them,' grumped Pierpont. 'And anyway I can't remember their names.'

Into the 1980s

Mrs Pierpont resumed her balaclava (in fact she hadn't missed a single purl or plain) and Pierpont decided to use the traditional method.

'Now there's Fido the Alsatian and Mandalay the Burmese and Tweetie . . . Pardon dear, but is the budgie still alive?'

'Yes,' said Mrs Pierpont without looking up. 'It was just the dengue fever that's been going around. Did I tell you what the ladies at the club are saying about it?'

'No, thank you,' said Pierpont, concentrating on the job in hand. 'That's me, you, Fido, Mandalay, Tweetie . . . we need two more. What are the names of the goldfish?'

But just then the butler entered to inform Pierpont that he was wanted desperately at the office of Blue Sky Mines, so Mrs Pierpont escaped into the fresh air of the living room while your correspondent made a hasty trip to town to attend to his directorial responsibilities.

When Pierpont reached the Blue Sky offices, young Penwiper, our poor but dishonest secretary, was in a state of high excitement.

'Sir,' he gasped as Pierpont limped goutily through the outer doors. 'We've got a security analyst.'

'Well I suppose that's better than dengue,' huffed Pierpont. 'But what do you mean "We've got one"?'

'A chap from a broker's office has called to assess the intrinsic value and future earnings of Blue Sky,' said Penwiper.

'Bless my soul!' exclaimed Pierpont. 'You're quite positive? He's not a liquidator or a receiver or something like that?'

'No, sir,' said Penwiper. 'He said "security analyst" quite clearly and he hadn't been drinking. He's from the broking firm of Runn and Ramp. They're quite small and I don't think they can afford many researchers.'

The light was slowly filtering through to Pierpont's brain. This might mean that the fine old company (founded 1970) might be about to be written up favourably in a broker's circular. This would be a milestone in Blue Sky's history because the only previous attention it had attracted from the broking fraternity had been confined to threatening letters from mercantile firms in regard to outstanding share trading accounts.

'What have you done with him?' asked Pierpont. 'What does he look like?'

'He's very young,' replied Penwiper. 'I gave him a large scotch and put him in the boardroom with Mr Bottle, who's been telling him all about the Last Card scheelite deposit.'

That made sense. Pierpont had heard Runn and Ramp had been having a lean time since the bottom fell out of the market. Only two weeks ago they had fired the mail room staff and you could tell the partners by their dry tongues because they spent half the day licking stamps. They probably could not afford any researchers except for those straight out of college.

Pierpont limped into the board room to find exactly the scene he had expected. Old Bottle, the geologist, was surrounded by geological maps and charts, waxing ecstatic about down-hole fluorescence to a glassy-eyed young man clutching a small vase full of Teachers.

As he shook hands, Pierpont decided the glazed look was only about half due to the scotch, and the rest to prolonged exposure to Bottle's views on Last Card. Of course, Bottle knows the true value of the deposit is a minus quantity but like all prospectors he likes to fantasise, and for once he had found a virginal audience.

'Have another drink,' beamed Pierpont, filling the lad's glass until the meniscus reached the rim. 'I don't think we've ever seen anyone from your firm here before.'

'No sir,' said the young fellow. 'My boss told me to do some research on Blue Metal Industries and I couldn't find them, but your name was the next on the share list and I thought you were probably associated.'

The lad's boss was obviously old, having failed to remember that Blue Metal had changed its name to BMI. And the lad was obviously green or he would no sooner have set foot in the Blue Sky offices than a sailor would board a ship flying the yellow quarantine flag.

'You've not been a researcher for long?' queried Pierpont, sitting quickly on a chair where the auditor's work sheets were laid out.

'Actually this is my first job,' the young chap said brightly. 'I've been doing night courses at the Securities Institute.'

Bottle beamed and laid a fatherly paw around the boy's shoulders. 'Don't worry about a thing,' he said. 'I'll even tell you about a couple of little prospects that the share market hasn't even guessed about yet.'

Well the share market hasn't guessed about the prospects, of course, because they don't exist. But the main thrust of the lad's review will be on the Last Card deposit which, Bottle whispered to him, had just been re-evaluated to contain two million tonnes of ore at 0.5 per cent.

'Gee, that sounds great,' exclaimed the lad. 'I suppose you'll be mining soon?'

'You can expect an announcement in the near future,' winked Bottle.

Pierpont glanced uneasily towards the ceiling and twitched his chair a little further from Bottle's. Your correspondent has never actually heard of a geologist being struck by a thunderbolt during an interview with a security analyst, but having been obliged to read a great deal of the Old Testament in his youth, Pierpont can never discount the possibility.

The fact is that an announcement on the mining of Last Card has been in the near future since the bond rate was 6 per cent. And while Last Card's reserves might sound impressive at first blush, Peko has 75 per cent more at the King Island Dolphin deposit alone at three times the grade and half a mile closer to the Earth's surface and even they're having trouble making an honest shilling. Not to mention that Last Card is far higher in impurities and more remote from civilisation.

Then Spender the accountant, obviously summoned by Penwiper, entered the boardroom and began talking to our young friend about future cash flows. He had moved on to the current share price (half buyer, one cent seller) being due to London jobbers shorting the stock at the start of the fortnightly account, when it occurred to Pierpont that if Jehovah felt moved to wrath he now had sufficient targets and anyway your correspondent had business elsewhere.

So he quietly bade farewell, after pouring the analyst another whisky, and headed for the ANZ registry with a bunch of off-market transfers in the name of Guppy and Goldie Pierpont.

It's taken a long time, but at last Mrs Pierpont's menagerie will be paying its way.

This will come as a complete surprise to you all, but there is still somebody left in Australia with a working knowledge of Scripture.

Following Pierpont's recent column, in which he expressed a fear that one day a geologist will be struck by one of Jehovah's thunderbolts while discussing his ore grades, your correspondent received a letter from Arthur Negus of Tuggerawong, NSW.

'Dear Pierpont,' he wrote, 'The ravages of time and alcohol have blurred your recollections of the Old Testament.'

'I've never actually read of anybody in the OT being struck by a thunderbolt. For every instance you can quote, I'll give $10 to the cats' home. Otherwise, you owe Jehovah an apology.'

Duck soup, thought Pierpont. The Old Testament must be rigid with thunderbolts. Those moggies in the cats' home had better stand by their bowls with their knives and forks because here come a few tins of Snappy Tom.

Arthur was right about the ravages senility has wrought upon Pierpont, however, because on closer inspection Pierpont could discover only one specific reference to thunderbolts and that was in Psalms 78:48, which reads: 'He gave up their cattle to the hail, and their flocks to hot thunderbolts.'

They must have done a roaring trade in doner kebabs that night, but Pierpont could see that flocks of sheep don't really count, so he tried again.

Dim memory told Pierpont that Jehovah had taken a personal dislike to King Herod. Your correspondent has never seen eye to eye with Jehovah on this point because, as they said of W.C. Fields, anyone who dislikes children can't be all bad, but Jehovah's viewpoint carried a bit more weight.

The Good Book tells us that Herod, arrayed in royal apparel, made such a great speech to the chaps in Tyre and Sidon that they thought he was a god.

'And immediately the angel of the Lord smote him, because he gave not God the glory: and he was eaten of worms, and gave up the ghost.'

Unfortunately, though, this is in the book of Acts, which is New Testament. And employing an angel as a hit-man probably doesn't count either.

Reflecting that the Israelis weren't the first chaps to do a bit of smiting around Tyre and Sidon, Pierpont turned to Exodus because the Egyptians were also on Jehovah's hit list.

Chapter nine tells how the Lord sent thunder and fire when Moses stretched forth his rod, but what he smote the Egyptians with, man and beast, was hail.

Jehovah, on all evidence, was a diversified smiter and did not rely on thunderbolts alone.

The evidence for this is in Deuteronomy 28, where Moses is giving a half-time pep talk to the Children of Israel and telling them what will happen if they don't play by the rules in the second half. Moses says: 'The Lord shall smite thee with a consumption, and with a fever, and with an inflammation, and with an extreme burning, and with the sword, and with blasting, and with mildew; and they shall pursue thee until thou perish.'

Pity, because otherwise Pierpont could have won the bet with Psalms 78:31, where the wrath of God came upon Jacob and the children of Ephraim 'and slew the fattest of them, and smote down the chosen men of Israel.' Might have been thunderbolts, but Arthur would probably argue it was mildew.

But your correspondent finally came up trumps with 1 Samuel 7:10, which is the tense bit about Samuel making a burnt offering as the Philistines draw near for battle. The Old Testament then says: 'But the Lord thundered with a great thunder on that day upon the Philistines, and discomfited them; and they were smitten before Israel.'

Well, if they were smitten during a thunderstorm, it must have been a thunderbolt, surely.

Send $10 to the cats' home, Arthur, while Pierpont retires to the Croesus Club for a plateful of burnt offering.

SIR MARK LENDS A HAND

The emergency board meeting started on an even more mendacious note than usual with Blue Sky's secretary Penwiper declaring that apologies had been received from the chairman, Sir Mark Time.

The truth was that the old dunderhead was absent because nobody had told him the meeting was on. Sir Mark's role in the company is purely as a figurehead and this was a meeting where its real state of affairs was to be discussed, so it was better that he be out of the way. Mind you, even if he had attended, the chances of Sir Mark discovering what was happening would have been remote — his skull being made of solid ivory.

Our problem was that the stock market boom in gold shares of early 1983 had caught Blue Sky napping. Spender had been skiing at Aspen; Bottle had been in jail at Marble Bar (drunk and disorderly on New Year's Eve); and Pierpont, working on the theory that the rally would not start until after the Newmarket, had flown to Monte Carlo for a flutter on the tables.

Consequently gold shares had begun running at a time when Blue Sky did not have a single gold prospect in its portfolio. Worse, it had not even announced it was about to acquire any.

The announcement was made as soon as Bottle had been bailed out by Penwiper ('. . . promising new areas, details of which will be disclosed soon'). The purpose of the board meeting was to make that statement true retrospectively.

Penwiper was the first to make a constructive suggestion.

'While Mr Bottle was . . . er . . . (he paused momentarily, seeking a tactful phrase) '. . . while Mr Bottle was out of the office, an old prospector named Harry Galena rang to offer us some gold prospects at Mt Magnet. Said we could have an option for $70,000 cash or $200,000 Blue Sky scrip at par.'

The offer had three drawbacks. First, the claims contained gold which made them expensive. Blue Sky far prefers barren claims, although they must be at a good address. Second, Harry Galena is not a chap whose business integrity inspires confidence. When the good Lord was handing out ethics, Harry was absent, doubtless salting a wolfram prospect. Third, he had found gold on this occasion only by overpegging a Very Big Company.

The case has received no publicity and is not due to come before the Warden's Court for a month but this is not a long time in which to ramp shares, and ugly, truthful rumours are always apt to leak out.

Blue Sky, of course has no moral quibbles about overpegging which is one of Australia's great traditional activities (after all, the whole of Australia is an overpegging of the original owners by Captain Cook) but Blue Sky prefers claim-jumping where it has a better chance of success than in Galena's case.

Bottle produced a nice prospect at Finke which had some promising surface indications of gold but we rejected it because it was not in a recognised gold-bearing district. It is high policy at Blue Sky (indeed, it is Blue Sky's only policy) that we do not mine the ground but the stock market, so we are only interested in fashionable addresses. It is an easier way of making money and infinitely less grubby.

The next logical step was to examine the possibility of salting one of our existing prospects. But almost the only prospect we had was the Last Card scheelite deposit, which has had more runs than Bernborough.

Back in the hysteria of the Poseidon days, one desperate company allegedly struck nickel in Western Australia and the shares ran for two days before anyone discovered that it was supposed to have been prospecting for zinc. But the market is more sceptical at present, so we reluctantly vetoed the idea of salting Last Card. It has been a severe test of investors' credulity to expect them to continue believing it is prospective for tungsten, let alone gold.

As we opened the second bottle of RD '70 Extra Brut, it was apparent that we were being driven into the arms of Galena. Pierpont poured himself a large draught, breathed deeply and rang old Harry.

'The price has gone up,' said Harry. 'A sucker has offered me $250,000 to buy it outright. Cash.'

'We can match that in Blue Sky scrip,' Pierpont retorted promptly.

Harry laughed like a hyena. 'No thanks,' he chortled. 'I wallpapered the bathroom last autumn.'

'Hang on a minute,' said Pierpont. 'How much cash do we have?' he whispered to Spender.

'Four hundred Ks from the rights issue,' Spender whispered back. 'But remember most of it's our money.'

The rights issue, on outrageous terms, was made while the market was low for the express purpose of squeezing out minority shareholders. Unbeknown to Sir Mark, the rest of the board, through its various nominees and Swiss bank accounts, now controlled some 90 per cent of Blue Sky. But that also meant we had to put cash into Blue Sky.

Pierpont held one hand over the phone while we had a quick caucus. Then we offered Harry $300,000.

'Give me five minutes and I'll let you know,' he said, and rang off.

'I hate spending real money,' muttered Spender. 'If he ups the ante, offer him an alternative. Tell him we'll wrap a prospectus around his claims and spin them off in a separate company. He can have as much equity as he likes but, of course, it will be escrow stock.'

Harry rang back. 'You've been outbid,' he declared.

Pierpont immediately offered him equity in a spin-off. 'No thanks,' he said. 'I've had some very nasty experiences with your vendor shares. And anyway, the other bidder offered $400,000 cash.'

'Get his signature on paper,' advised Pierpont. 'Before the asylum discovers he's escaped.' He hung up.

After a moment's silence, Spender asked wearily: 'Okay, how much is Finke?'

'About fifty,' said Bottle. 'But I'll have to leave now to catch the plane. And you won't be able to contact me because it's way out in the bush.'

'All right,' sighed Spender. 'If we don't have a gold prospect somewhere in our portfolio it will be like losing our citizenship.'

Bottle grabbed his overnight bag, which he keeps in the boardroom for these occasions, tucked a bottle of Bolly under one arm and ran out of the room.

The rest of us had another drink and were halfway through drafting a statement to the stock exchange ('The innovative board of Blue Sky Mines NL has opened an exciting new gold province ...') when in walked a beaming Sir Mark.

'Board meeting, eh?' he chuckled jovially. 'Sorry, I must have forgotten. But I've been working a bit too, you know.'

He sat down and lit a satisfied Ramon Allones. 'I've picked up a gold prospect at Mount Magnet from old Harry Galena. He rang me at the Croesus Club and offered it to me. Had to bid like the devil to get it, too.'

He blew a fat smoke ring. 'I'm afraid I've rather used up our cash,' he said. 'But we can always have another issue, can't we? Eh, what?'

The Official History of Blue Sky Mines

TECHNICAL BRIEF 2

HOW TO SPOT A HIGH-RISK COMPANY

One of the difficulties facing your average ignorant investor is how – given the hundreds of mining stocks listed on Australian bourses – he can tell a legitimate junior miner from one of the Blue Sky variety.

After all, if he buys into some earnest company toiling away diligently at a mineral sand deposit, the stock will never move. Nor will our investor find any useful guide in the official literature of speculative companies, which portrays them all as pocket editions of Western Mining, applying high technology and even higher integrity to the exploitation of orebodies.

The secret is that you can tell a speculative company by WHAT THE PROMOTERS SAY ABOUT IT. For these purposes, the term 'promoter' includes any broker or tipster associated with the stock. The following list of key phrases has been compiled by Pierpont with considerable assistance from Melbourne mining consultant Jack Sturgess. Pierpont can guarantee that the list is definitive, several of the phrases having doubtless been used in the South Australian copper boom of the 1840s.

People
1. 'He used to be a bit fleet of foot, but he's reformed now.' (This one is an infallible guide. If your broker tells you this about a promoter, don't even bother checking the rest of the list.)
2. 'The mine's owned by this syndicate of dentists.'
3. (About an accountant) 'He's the best explorer in the business.'
4. (About a promoter) 'He doesn't know anything about mining, geology or economics, but he sure knows the business.'
5. 'The vendor seems a reasonable guy.' (He wasn't in jail when I met him.)

Assays
6. 'Only one assayer can grade this one correctly.' (None of the others went to the same night school.)
7. 'We lost values in the drilling water.' (Ore grades are always lowered, never enhanced, by sampling techniques. This is an iron law of speculative exploration.)

The deposit
8. 'We have this high-grade deposit in the West.' (But how large?)
9. 'We have this large deposit in the West.' (But what grade?)
10. 'We have this large high-grade deposit in the Central African Republic.'
11. 'The old stock route is where the diamonds really are.' (Once – it may have been at Coolgardie – two prospectors discovered that the old camel route through the claims had never been dug. They pegged it and extracted nice gold values. Ever since then, every stock route has been a mine.)
12. 'We have a good title, free and clear.' (The over-pegging case starts on Monday.)

Water
13. 'They couldn't handle water in those days.' (No old mine could ever handle the water table and a lot of existing mines have trouble with it, but it is never going to be a problem in any speculative mine. This is another iron law of speculative mining.)
14. 'The workings have been flooded for 100 years, but it won't need anything except pumps.' (And, just possibly, many kilometres of careful rock-bolting.)
15. 'Modern pumps will handle it.' (See 13.)
16. 'You'll never believe this, but although the dredge has been floating there for 40 years without maintenance, there isn't a speck of rust on it because of the constant rain.'

Discovery
17. 'An old-timer told me . . .' (He was in an asylum.)
18. 'It's never been drilled.' (Mainly because it's granite.)
19. 'They never drilled where the high grade is.' (It's high-grade granite.)
20. 'The Abos wouldn't tell the Poms where it was.' (Yet it's so rich in uranium it's supposed to glow in the dark.)
21. 'The chopper pilots spotted some old diggings on what we thought was the wrong side of the fault zone.' (This one should be treated with caution. At least one genuine mine was discovered in this fashion.)
22. 'Our geologist has made a complete reinterpretation of the old Mount Fuzzlewit field. Brilliant work for a lad.' (We found it by sheer luck.)

The Official History of Blue Sky Mines

23. 'The hole finished in ore.' (We weren't game to drill another inch.)

What the majors missed

(If you value your peace of mind, <u>never</u> check any of these statements with the company concerned.)

24. 'Esso tested the wrong zones.' (Funny, they still spent a million on wire logs.)
25. De Beers drilled and said there was nothing because they didn't want to flood the market with the diamonds.' (Even more cunningly, De Beers then abandoned the leases.)
26. 'CRA pegged too far to the west and didn't know what they were doing.'
27. 'BHP's mining division liked it, but the top brass thought it was too small.' (It will only make $5 million next year.)
28. 'Peko tested for copper instead of nickel.'
29. 'Amax walked away from it because of politics.'
30. 'Minsec delineated the orebody, then ran out of money.' (An asset the liquidator never noticed.)
31. 'MIM were only considering open cut and never drilled at depth.'

Special advantages

32. 'It carries platinum values as well.' (All speculative deposits carry platinum values. This is a third iron law.)
33. '... And it's got rare earths.' (Not to mention vanadium.)
34. 'She gets wider and richer with depth.' (Beyond present drilling levels, that is.)
35. 'We've developed a special leaching process.' (It worked on 2 cc in the lab.)
36. To be conservative, we haven't attributed any value to the antimony.' (Which in this case happens to be an impurity.)

Finance and economics

37. 'We have developed a new extraction technique which halves costs.' (Completely new – it's never been tried anywhere else on the planet.)
38. 'The government stamp batteries will crush it cheaply.' (Only six months' wait, too.)
39. '... And when oil gets to $40 a barrel this new technology will make our deposit viable ...' (Substitute any other metal or hydrocarbon at slightly above prevailing prices.)

Into the 1980s

If you have heard any four of the above 39 statements about your company, it is speculative. The same applies if you have heard only statement 1, or any two out of 6, 16, 22, 29 and 32. If you have hear more than six of the above statements, send Pierpont the prospectus immediately.

PIERPONT'S & COLOURING —

RULE 1: ALL DIRECTORS FAILING THIS TEST ARE
RULE 2: BRING YOUR OWN CRAYONS

QUESTIONS

① WHAT IS YOUR NAME?

A. ALAN BOND
B. IDI AMIN
C. DONALD DUCK
D. NAPOLEON
E. ALL OF THE ABOVE

CORRECT ANSWER: LOSE 5 I.Q POINTS

③ WHICH PICTURE IS OUT OF PLACE?

CORRECT ANSWER ✓

④ YOU HAVE JUST SPENT 5 MINUTES WORKING FOR YOUR COMPANY
— WHAT FEE SHOULD YOU CHARGE?

A. $5,000
B. $50,000
C. $500,000
D. $5,000,000

CORRECT ANSWER: TAKE VENDOR SHARES AS A BONUS

② WHERE DO YOU LIVE?

A. WITH MY MUM
B. CELL 4091
C. ON A LEAR JET
D. BATTLESTAR GALACTICA

CORRECT ANSWER: HAVE A SWEETIE

⑤ SHOULD DIRECTORS BE OVER PAID?

A. YES
B. ABSOLUTELY
C. AND INDEMNIFIED

CORRECT ANSWER: TAKE VENDOR OPTIONS TOO

GIANT I.Q. TEST IN BOOK!

GUARANTEED IMMUNITY FROM PROSECUTION
TIME: TO BE COMPLETED IN 12 MONTHS LESS TIME OFF FOR GOOD BEHAVIOUR

6 YOUR PRIVATE COMPANY HAS JUST BOUGHT AN EXPLORATION LEASE FOR $10,000. AT WHAT PRICE SHOULD YOU SELL IT TO THE PUBLIC COMPANY YOU CONTROL?
A. $10,000
B. $1M
C. 50% FOR $2M PLUS MANAGEMENT FEES
CORRECT ANSWER: GIVE HALF TO PIERPONT

7 THIS IS YOUR BOARDROOM

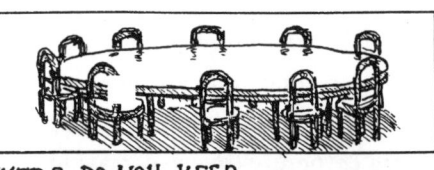

WHERE DO YOU KEEP...
A. THE BLONDE
B. THE BOLLINGER
C. NEXT YEARS SIGNED AUDIT
D. THE SHREDDER

(USE DIFFERENT CRAYONS FOR EACH ANSWER)
CORRECT ANSWER: LOSE 500 I.Q. POINTS

8 CAN YOU SPELL "DIV-I-D-END"?
A. NO
B. NO
THERE IS ONLY ONE CORRECT ANSWER

9 HOW MUCH DOES ONE OF THESE COST?
A. $1M
B. $2M
C. THE COMPANY PAYS
CORRECT ANSWER LOSE 60 I.Q. POINTS

10 WHERE DO YOU FILE TAX RETURNS?
A. ZUG
B. COOK ISLANDS
C. JERSEY
D. WHAT TAX RETURN?
CORRECT ANSWER GO TO THE DUTCH ANTILLES

11 WHAT IS THIS PICTURE?

A. PORT DOUGLAS
B. MAJORCA
C. HEAD OFFICE
CORRECT ANSWER: LOSE 900,000,000,000

3
THE BOOM YEARS
~

*I*n *1983 the Labor Party won office, deregulated the financial markets and the markets quickly emerged from the short Fraser recession into a raging boom. Stupid banks loaned stupid amounts of money to stupid corporate cowboys, raising the share prices of stupid companies to stupid levels.*

The all ordinaries index more than quadrupled in the four years after 1983, hitting a peak of 2312 in September 1987.

The main action was in the stocks of the corporate cowboys and their takeover targets, the biggest game being the rival efforts of John Elliott and Robert Holmes à Court to take over BHP. Companies such as Bond Corporation and Ariadne did huge deals in quick, dizzying succession. Small speculative companies were a secondary game and many of them had a bumpy ride on the back of the gold price, which slumped from $US500 an ounce at the start of 1983 to under $US300 at the start of 1985 then surged back to $US500 just before the market crash in 1987.

Corporate crime was sternly policed by the NCSC under Henry Bosch.

IN BLUE SKY WE TRUST

Studying the board of Blue Sky Mines as they gathered for their June meeting, Pierpont reflected that it was just as well that modern communications have not yet advanced to the point where shareholders can watch the directors of their companies.

Blue Sky's shareholders only ever see the stock exchange quotations and the mailed annual accounts (which always arrive the day after the annual meeting). If they ever saw the directors, they would sell in mass panic.

Pierpont's rheumy eyes and inflamed nose would by themselves be enough to deter the average investor and he looks positively handsome alongside Bottle the geologist, who has spent the last 60 years clambering around spinifex and drinking with prospectors and drilling contractors.

Our chairman, Sir Mark Time, looks like a remnant from the last Cabinet of William Ewart Gladstone. Spender the accountant looks old and furtive and Penwiper the secretary looks young and furtive. On sight, not a group you would trust with the custody of an old pair of sandshoes but, sight unseen, widows and orphans entrust their life savings to us. As P.T. Barnum said, there's one born every minute.

The first item on the agenda was to serve Sir Mark with a large Glenfiddich, thereby ensuring he went bang off to sleep. We had serious business to discuss and as long as Sir Mark was conscious there was always the chance, admittedly a deep outside one, that his mind might slip into gear and he would realise what his fellow directors were doing.

We prefer to keep him as a purely figurehead chairman, not because we suspect him of possible honesty but because he is too poorly equipped with guile to run a modern Australian speculative company. Or to put it another way, he'd get caught.

In fairness, Pierpont must confess that not even Sir Mark could have done worse than the rest of the board recently. Back in April when the all ords was 760 and the future was bright we formed a little spin-off called Hot Rock Mining No Liability.

It was typical of a present-day float. We loaded it with a few old dogs of properties and charged as high a cash consideration for them as the NCSC would wear.

Blue Sky then subscribed for 40 per cent of the float, intending to stag the stock as soon as Hot Rock listed. In mid-stream we were caught by a medium-sized apocalypse when the Dow Jones dropped vertically. By the time the Blue Sky board met, the all ords was down to 680 and worse, Hot Rock shares had come on below par.

Blue Sky had never paid for its Hot Rock shares, intending to slip the funds across after stagging. Not being vendor scrip, they are disposable, but how? One way would be by talking up the stock.

'I don't suppose any of these prospects are actually worth anything?' Spender mused, idly thumbing through the Hot Rock prospectus which none of us had read. 'What's this big lead-zinc deposit in the Northern Territory, for instance?'

'It wasn't viable in the '60s, so I don't see why it should be now,' replied Bottle.

'The gold prospect at Nullagine has a good address.'

'Sold to us by an old prospector called Wacka,' said Bottle. 'I think he pulled a swifty on us because it seems to have been pegged first by a couple of other companies. We're trying to keep quiet about that one.'

'Well at least we have the other gold mine at Wiluna,' said Spender. 'A consulting geo signed a reserve statement on that one.'

Pierpont winced as Bottle told the painful story. The geo concerned had been in the Leonora pub for a week at the time and was under the impression that he was Benito Mussolini signing the Lateran Treaty. This caused no small disruption to the social life of the town because it had the temporary effect of making the public bar holy ground and incoming thirsty locals had been barred from entry until they could produce their visas.

So we're following another modern trend. Blue Sky will raise a bank loan, pledged on various assets such as Pierpont's cellar, then form a trust, put the borrowings and the shares in it and get the whole disaster off the balance sheet. If the technique's good enough for CSR with Delhi Petroleum, it's good enough for us.

The meeting was declared closed and we trudged off to the Croesus Club, leaving Penwiper to awaken Sir Mark.

CAUGHT SHORT WITH A VAULTFUL OF DOLLARS

The attendance cheques having been handed out, the board meeting of Blue Sky Mines was declared open. Present were Sir Mark Time, Pierpont, Bottle, Spender and Penwiper.

The presence of Sir Mark was, as usual, a great handicap to frank and free discussion. Comatose as Sir Mark is, there is always a chance – roughly equal to being hit by a falling meteorite – that the old drone might stumble across the larcenous plans of the rest of us and have a cardiac arrest or, worse, a spasm of honesty. 'Seems a long time since I was at one of these meetings,' Sir Mark mused, thumbing through the minutes. 'I must have missed the last few notifications.'

Pierpont took a long draw on his Ramon Allones and blew a smoke ring toward the ceiling. The reason Sir Mark missed the meetings was that we had not bothered to call any since the Melbourne Cup. To comply with the Companies Act, there have been minutes of meetings entered by Penwiper, who took Honours in Minute Forging when he gained his secretary's certificate (which was also forged).

'Looking back over the minutes, we don't seem to have done much since that call a year ago,' observed Sir Mark. 'What did we do with the money again?'

'We raised a million from the shareholders,' Spender reminded him, 'And spent half of it on the Dying Dingo gold deposit.'

Quite true, as far as it went. But that was not very far.

The full truth was that, at the end of 1983 – sensing the return to life of the speculative market – Spender, Bottle and Pierpont had decided to tighten their hold on Blue Sky and clean out unwanted minority shareholders by the classical mechanism of a call on the partly paid shares. This is a routine operation. The three of us have made a handsome living over the years by selling our stock on market during Blue Sky's buoyant periods, then cleaning out the small shareholders with a call or a capital reconstruction when the market falls again. A historical graph of Blue Sky's capital shows it expanding and contracting like a concertina in direct ratio to the share price.

A harmless pastime and socially useful, because it mops up excess money that shareholders might otherwise spend on luxuries such as food and rent.

This time, the tactic misfired because something like three-quarters of the outside shareholders were silly enough to pay their calls and Blue Sky wound up with a million in the banks for the first time in living memory.

Worse, Pierpont, Bottle and Spender, seeing the money come in, had to pay calls themselves to maintain their effective half-interest in the company, so half of the million dollars was ours.

We promptly recovered the money by buying Dying Dingo for half a million from a Vanuatu company whose ancestry can be traced through a string of trusts in Liechtenstein, Switzerland and Jersey – but only by a Corporate Affairs inspector prepared to spend the whole year's budget on travel.

The real owners of Dying Dingo were, of course, the three of us.

'Ah, yes! Dying Dingo looked quite promising, didn't it,' Sir Mark recalled. 'And I see we've spent several thousand dollars exploring it, Bottle.'

As Bottle launched into a description of Dying Dingo laced with every technical expression he could remember, Pierpont groped for the decanter of Glendronach.

In truth, we had spent several thousand dollars exploring the cellars of the Croesus Club and nary a penny on Dying Dingo. When we bought, the deposit was generally understood to contain a large but unspecified tonnage of auriferous ore grading slightly over a gram to the tonne. Superficially, it looks as though we might have a viable open-cut gold mine. But there are a couple of metallurgical problems, notably the presence of low-grade stibnite. This is the ore of antimony. Gold and antimony will combine in the concentrate during the treatment and can be separated only at great cost. We plan to let the stock exchange know about this somewhere around 2000.

'Well, I can see Dying Dingo will take a while to evaluate,' said Sir Mark, as Bottle's tirade wound down. 'But what are we doing with the rest of the money?'

'We deposited it with Westpac,' said Spender. 'Can't be too careful, you know.'

In the long pause while Sir Mark tried to remember who Westpac were (he'll still be calling it the Bank of New South Wales next century), Pierpont reflected that we were reaching high levels of mendacity today even by Blue Sky's standards.

The money had been on deposit for the flicker of an eyelid before Blue Sky had begun punting the foreign exchange market.

If we had consulted economists, we would have gone long on the $A at 81c. Having never consulted an economist about an investment decision in our lives, we went short in November and stayed short.

We saw this as our patriotic duty, on the grounds that we were thickening the market in the national currency and obviously complying with the tacit wishes of the Reserve Bank, which has been refusing to prop the currency by buying dollars.

In the process we have netted – after tax and brokerage – another million dollars.

For the first time in the company's chequered career, the directors of Blue Sky are in grave peril of paying a dividend to shareholders, but we think we can get rid for the money.

The most fashionable way of doing this is by buying an invention and floating a high-technology company. Blue Sky is falling in with the trend. The name will be Sky High Tech Ltd and it is to be launched any day now with a vendor consideration of $1.5 million. Blue Sky will hold 51 per cent of Sky High Tech and the public will hold 49. Pierpont, Spender and Bottle will hold the vendor consideration.

Having decided on the name and the vendor consideration, we have determined the two most important factors for any high-tech venture. What it will actually invent is an administrative detail which can be discussed in due course. From the recent share market success of Vapocure, Sarich and Gene Link, it will probably be something that injects paint into genes.

And there will be loads of uncalled liability on the shares.

GOLDEN PILLARS OF SALT

The chairman, that old dodderer Sir Mark Time, passed the box of Upmann coronas to Pierpont and declared open the board meeting of Blue Sky Mines.

Pierpont had ample time to pierce his corona, light it lovingly and reach for the Glendronach decanter while Sir Mark pondered the agenda. Our chairman's mental processes work at the speed of a

The Official History of Blue Sky Mines

glacier in bottom gear and Pierpont has sometimes advanced well into his second Upmann before Sir Mark has finished cogitating.

At yesterday's meeting, however, Pierpont had barely accumulated half an inch of ash when Sir Mark said: 'There's only one item on the agenda: "Float Glittering Gold Mines No Liability". What does it mean?'

What it means, as readers will have guessed, is that the other geriatric directors of Blue Sky are planning yet another robbery of the investing public.

Spender the accountant perceived a couple of months ago that the share prices of heavyweight gold producers were tending to rise faster than the speculatives. Overseas investors, becoming nervous about the prospects of South African gold mines, were switching into Australian golds. But as these investors have big chunks of money they were necessarily limited to larger company with lots of shares, such as Kidston and Western Mining.

Spender therefore suggested we should form a gold mining company with 200 million shares so that all the punters in London, New York and Zurich had something to buy. 'If the rest of the world wants to buy Australian mining shares, I see it as our international duty to supply some,' he declared.

So we ran off the scrip – tastefully engraved, because Blue Sky believes in upholding standards for the wallpaper trade – and kept a little over 50 per cent for ourselves as vendor stock, in line with current market practice.

'Well, I suppose if everybody else is taking that percentage, it must be all right,' said Sir Mark. 'How many gold mines do we have?'

'Two,' replied Bottle the geologist. Pierpont inched his chair a little further from Bottle's. If God happened to be listening, He might well have aimed a thunderbolt at Bottle on the strength of that monosyllable and Pierpont did not want to be too close when it happened.

But the Big Speculator in the Sky was apparently not paying attention or – more probably – had given away the Blue Sky board as a lost cause, because no thunderbolts arrived even though Bottle was talking about the Bonanza Creek open cut.

The Boom Years

Bonanza Creek is an ancient buried river bed in north Queensland. The miners simply scrape the surface waste away, expose the old river gravels and dig the alluvials out in a straightforward operation.

Spender, Bottle and Pierpont bought Bonanza Creek from the locals for $100,000 and have sold it to Glittering Gold Mines for $10 million in vendor shares. Our control of this asset is, as you would expect, camouflaged by a variety of trusts and companies in Liberia, Grand Cayman, Monaco and the Isle of Man.

'Why, the figures look quite good,' burbled Sir Mark. 'And judging by the map, the strike length could continue for miles. All the drillholes show the gravels continue. Excellent, excellent.'

As Sir Mark has never understood a drilling grid in his life there was little danger that he would question this one. A careful scrutiny of the forward drilling would show that the gravels only last at the present depth for about the next 20 metres. After that, the very few reported drillholes show the river gravels continuing, but at 10 times the present depth.

Somewhere just ahead of the present pit limit at Bonanza Creek we are going to run into the ancient Bonanza Waterfall, which drops vertically by something like the height of the Rialto building. It must have been an impressive sight a few million years ago: one of the area's leading tourist attractions. Aborigines and dinosaurs probably took package tours from Moonee Ponds to see it.

As a modern mine, it will be hopelessly uneconomic. The waste-ore ratio will shoot up to ten to one and the grade is not high enough to justify underground mining. We therefore expect Bonanza Creek to cut out production about a month after listing.

The second gold mine is Drongo Deeps, an operation in Western Australia which was last worked in the 1930s. Bottle, Pierpont and Spender are again the secret vendors.

Two diamond drillholes have been sunk here. The first had an intersection at 20 ft assaying 30 grams to the tonne. The second showed 40 ft of eight gram material.

'Very promising,' exclaimed Sir Mark. 'Obviously we have to raise money from the public to spend on further exploration of this project.'

Actually diamond drill hole number one was a nasty shock to us all. For several days we thought we might have a real mine on our hands.

This would have been an historic and unwelcome occurrence at Blue Sky. Mining requires effort and expenditure and is risky financially, physically and politically. Blue Sky prefers to mine the share market and thereby enable its directors to live in the more civilised bits of the continent.

Anyhow, Bottle, shocked into sobriety, did some careful measuring and examination of old mine plans and discovered that by a sheer fluke we had drilled a pillar.

When old-time miners were working on a large orebody underground they did not dig it all out. They had to leave some of the ore standing in pillars because otherwise the roof would have fallen in. Our drill had gone vertically through one of the old pillars. A few inches to the left or right and we would have logged 20 ft of fresh air, or more probably water. All of the rest of the one ounce gold had been dug out by the old-timers.

This was confirmed by the second drillhole, which encountered no gold at all in the first trial cores sent to the assay lab. Bottle then salted the rest of the core and sent that to the lab, which duly analysed it as eight gram gold.

Drongo Deeps therefore stands in the prospectus as a superbly promising prospect, but don't hold your breath waiting for drillhole number three because it is never going to happen.

Meanwhile, if you run into anyone from Zurich looking for Australian gold shares, we have them lying around Blue Sky's office in heaps.

WHAT'S A FEW NOUGHTS BETWEEN FRIENDS?

Leo Liability the stockbroker and Pierpont were down at the bourse the other day, trying to outguess the market on Holmes à Court's next move in BHP options, when your correspondent noted a couple of traders bidding an obscure stock on the speculative board.

The Boom Years

Having committed enough on July $9.50s to win a small sheep station, Pierpont felt he could afford to relax with a few side bets.

'What's happening over there?' he asked Leo.

'You should know,' grunted Leo. 'They're bidding up Blue Sky Mines.'

'Incredible,' breathed Pierpont, but sure enough they were. The old stock had gone to six cents, which is at least seven-and-a-half above its intrinsic value. Only a couple of weeks earlier they had been half a cent seller and the company in such hopeless condition that Pierpont had stopped looking at their market.

'You might have given me the tip,' snorted Leo. 'I'd just bailed all my clients out of the stock when Blue Sky came out with a strong set of accounts.' We retreated to his trading desk and he handed over his copy of the annual report. 'See what I mean?' he said.

Well it *was* our annual report – with a plain blue cover (we daren't show shareholders a photo of the Last Card scheelite mine) and inside a fulmination from the directors on international metal price trends (plagiarised from *Business Week*) and the 'true and fair' teddy bear stamp from the auditor, which he had signed in return for a trip to inspect our $2 subsidiary in Monte Carlo.

But the bit of the report with the numbers in it did not seem familiar.

Pierpont is highly conversant with Blue Sky's state of affairs because we have spent a great deal of our waking time since June 30 trying to find some way of disguising them.

Under the influence of strong liquor, the directors decided last February to go long in tin and short the yen. The result was catastrophic. We lost more than a million and finished the year with a deficiency on shareholders' funds of about $400,000.

By stretching generally accepted accounting principles like elastic, we managed to diminish the apparent damage by about 30 per cent but our accounts were still ghastly.

Pierpont could still remember the final board meeting a month earlier when we pushed the papers outlining this financial apocalypse across to Penwiper, our poor but dishonest secretary, and told him to send it off to the printers.

The rest of the annual report had been there for weeks awaiting the balance sheet, profit and loss account and notes. If we did not

The Official History of Blue Sky Mines

issue the accounts soon, while all the Borals and Repcos and Brambles were still coming out, we would be one of the lonely tail-enders emerging in December and much more visible to financial scribes looking for somebody new to insult.

The report had hit the streets a fortnight ago and Pierpont had not bothered to open his copy. Nor, fortunately, had any else. The event had passed unnoticed by the financial world.

Or *almost* unnoticed. One or two analysts must have looked at the figures long enough to think it was a buy. The numbers in the Blue Sky annual report bore no relation to the ones Pierpont had spent so many hours trying to distort.

The company showed a profit of a quarter of a million (on share trading, dividends and interest) and had more than a million in cash and short-term deposits. And the issued capital seemed to have about doubled.

Deeply puzzled, Pierpont limped goutily around to the Blue Sky Mines boardroom to find that Penwiper, Spender and Bottle were already in session.

'What happened?' inquired Pierpont, waving the annual report.

'We're just getting to the bottom of it,' replied Spender. 'You realise that poor Penwiper has been under stress lately.'

A nice euphemism. Penwiper went long on tin on his own account and, at the last reckoning, had lost the equivalent of five mortgages on his home. The strain of keeping this news from Mrs Penwiper, a beautiful but avaricious young harpy, had driven Penwiper to drink. Pierpont remembered he had been at least three sheets into the wind the night we gave him the accounts to send to the printers. In any ordinary company he would have been sacked, but he knows a few too many secrets for Blue Sky to let him go and anyhow it would set an undesirable precedent if alcoholism became a sacking offence at Blue Sky.

'You know that our printers, Thumbprint and Spindle, do the accounts for a number of other speculative companies?' said Spender. 'Well, it appears that Penwiper had the idea of bribing a press hand to get proofs of their accounts. If he found anything worthwhile, he would buy or sell the stock and get square on his tin disaster.'

The Boom Years

'Very bright,' said Pierpont admiringly. 'Did he get out of jail?'

'On the financial side, yes,' said Spender. 'Perhaps you had better explain the rest, Penwiper.'

'Well sir, the night you gave me the Blue Sky accounts, I still had a bundle of stolen ones with me,' explained Penwiper. 'I shredded them to destroy the evidence before I sent ours to the printers but ... er ... I was a little distracted that night and I think I shredded ours and sent someone else's to the printers.'

It took a full half-minute for this to sink in. Then Pierpont understood.

'You mean,' he croaked. 'That we've issued our annual report with someone else's accounts in it?'

'Er ... yes, sir,' mumbled Penwiper, standing on one leg. Spender poured Pierpont a stiff Teachers as your correspondent tottered into a chair.

'Who knows?' gasped Pierpont.

'Just us, so far,' replied Spender.

'Whose accounts were they?'

'Er, I've forgotten sir,' said Penwiper, shifting to the other leg. 'And there's no way we can trace them.'

'Pity,' said Bottle. 'They look so healthy, I wouldn't mind buying a few.'

A long silence ensued while Pierpont lowered his Teachers and poured himself another five fingers.

'We could try telling the truth,' mused Spender. This, of course, was purely a conversational gambit. Truth has never been company policy at Blue Sky. And Pierpont doubts whether it would be well received. He closed his eyes and tried to picture the scene:

Pierpont enters Henry Bosch's office, lights him a cigar and slaps him on the back.

Pierpont: Blue Sky Mines has just issued a false balance sheet. Simple mistake, you know, and we're frightfully sorry.

Henry: (nonchalantly) Thanks for telling me, old chap. Are you going to issue a correct one?

Pierpont: Afraid we can't. Lost the figures in the shredder, don't you know.

Henry: These little slips will happen. Ha ha ha ha (laughs jovially). Lucky we've got a sense of humour here at the NCSC, eh? Ho ho ho. How about a spot of lunch at my club?

Pierpont could not quite put his finger on it, but there seemed to be something wrong with this script. And, if Henry didn't happen to be in the office, could Pierpont rely on the other chaps at the NCSC to take the same sporting attitude?

If they started a full-scale investigation of Blue Sky, who knows what skeletons might be uncovered?

'Or we could just sit tight,' suggested Bottle.

Not as silly as it sounds. With the mountain of annual reports rolling through the stock exchanges and the NCSC at this time of year, a small explorer is hardly worth a second glance — especially as speculative company accounts are relatively meaningless. If anyone compares our 1984 figures in our 1984 and 1985 accounts, we shall have to think of a good explanation for the divergence but so far nobody has. We could always dummy next year's accounts so that 1985 could be brought into line.

'What about the auditor?' asked Pierpont. 'I take it we did the usual deal and he had to sign the accounts before we gave him the airline ticket.'

'He always signs with his eyes shut,' said Penwiper. 'He says he feels happier that way.'

Pierpont could follow the psychology.

'Taking the broad view,' your correspondent said. 'I suppose that a balance sheet is just a snapshot of a company in time and, at some point in time, our accounts will look like the ones we've presented.'

'They will be by next June, anyway,' promised Spender, who got his PhD in post-balance-date adjustments.

'So all we've got wrong is the date, then. And that's hardly a thing the authorities would want to be worried about, eh? I think it would save them a lot of bother if we just kept this to ourselves.'

'Agreed,' chorused the rest.

Just don't tell anyone you read about it here, that's all.

The Boom Years

BLUE SKY DISCOVERS PLATINUM

Looking at the evil, grinning faces around him, Pierpont decided he had never seen such a smug board of directors. The board of Blue Sky Mines (No Liability Except At Gunpoint) has been prospering during the gold boom.

Bottle the geologist has been making sinful amounts of money. All his old cronies from faraway pubs such as the Ironclad at Marble Bar and the Palace at Kalgoorlie keep giving him the nod or the whisper from the field with the result that he has been making one killing after another as an insider in the gold stocks.

Spender the accountant and Pierpont have also made handsome profits as insiders, with the important difference that we have been trading in Blue Sky. Blue Sky bought the Roca Solada (Spanish for 'salted rock') claims near Broad Arrow.

The claims were brought to Pierpont and Spender by old Harry Galena the prospector and your correspondent will not soon forget the negotiating session over the price.

'Thought I'd do you a favour,' said Harry. 'I noticed Blue Sky didn't have anything it could call a gold mine so I pegged Roca Solada.'

'As you know, it's barren quartz and you could dig through to the earth's core without finding a pennyweight, but someone salted a few feet of it in the old days and sold it to an English syndicate who dug a small hole before finding out they'd been diddled, so I suppose you could call it a mine.'

'How much?' asked Spender.

'Well, we should put a bit of a price on it so it looks fair dinkum,' said Harry. 'Er . . . what about . . . um' (he shuffled his feet) 'Perhaps . . . . er . . . $25,000?' He blushed slightly.

'No,' smiled Spender. '$50,000.'

Harry's jaw fell slack, as though he doubted both his sanity and his hearing.

'Twenty-five for you and a procuration fee of twenty-five for Pierpont and me,' explained Spender.

A gleam of intelligence returned to Harry's eye. 'Blue Sky gives me a cheque for fifty and I give both of you a cheque for twenty-five?' he asked.

'Payable to a Panamanian trust account,' added Spender.

'Done,' said Harry.

That piece of larceny settled, Spender and Pierpont spent the next month mopping up Blue Sky stock, which was only a few cents at the time.

Then we sent news filtering around the market that Blue Sky was acquiring an old mine and the stock soared. Then we sold our holdings, shorted an extra million for luck, and announced a call.

The share price fell again like a stone. We will probably spend the rest of the year answering queries from the NCSC, but it has been richly rewarding.

Looking at the rest of the board table, Penwiper, our poor but dishonest secretary, is winning for once. Penwiper, whose unwise speculations keep him on the brink of debtors' prison, went long in gold six months ago. The futures market has risen to the point where even he was unable to avoid making a profit.

And our dunderheaded chairman, Sir Mark Time, is happy. Rumours that the Melbourne Establishment are going to buy Holmes à Court out of BHP have given him a satisfied smile, which he was still wearing when he opened the Blue Sky board meeting.

'The only item on the agenda is Roca Solada,' he said. 'I take it we're going to start a mine there?'

We all winced. The old fool has sat on the Blue Sky board for 15 years now without realising it is high policy that the company does not dig holes in the ground. That is a high-risk occupation and too seldom rewarded. We prefer to mine the market, which is closer to civilisation anyway.

'I think that might be premature,' said Spender, the first to recover speech. 'We're undertaking an exploration program first.'

'I've been taking some selected soil samples,' said Bottle.

Highly selected, to say the least. Bottle believes in extremely scientific exploration, in the sense that he always knows exactly what the result of his exploration program will be. In this case he bought a couple of rings from a jeweller's shop, ground them to fine dust and sprinkled it into the samples from half a dozen small holes.

'Excellent,' said Sir Mark. 'Do we have any results yet?'

'The assays are only preliminary,' replied Bottle. 'But we look like having around half a gram of platinum to the tonne.' Bottle chose platinum rings because gold is becoming rather common.

'Magnificent!' exclaimed Sir Mark. 'Do we have enough money for more exploration?'

'We raised enough in the call,' said Spender.

'But I thought that failed?' said Sir Mark.

'It was underwritten, sir,' said Penwiper, 'By some trust in Panama.'

Spender looked at the ceiling. Pierpont contemplated the oil painting of Carlo Ponzi on the east wall. We are set for the big rise when the market learns Blue Sky is a platinum stock.

'So we have money too,' burbled Sir Mark. 'We can start a platinum mine.'

'It might be better – after we release the sample assays – to float Roca Solada as a separate company,' advised Spender.

'Platinum's for floating, not for mining,' said Bottle.

A puzzled crease furrowed Sir Mark's brow for a moment, then cleared. 'That's for you technical chaps to worry about,' he said. 'But as everything seems to be going well, why don't I shout you fellows to lunch at the Croesus Club?'

Spender's smile was smugger than ever. 'In the circumstances,' he beamed, 'I think we can afford to shout you, Sir Mark.'

PLAYING THE LAST CARD

A quorum of the directors being sober, the first board meeting of Blue Sky Mines No Liability for 1987 was declared open.

Indeed, it may well have been the first board meeting for 1986 as well, because Pierpont is stretched to recall the last time that the directors sat down at a formal meeting with the minute book on the table.

Blue Sky has been quite active in this time, of course. It has been buying gold prospects, ramping stocks on the share market, creating exotic new breeds of preference share, sending directors to lengthy seminars in the Bahamas, bribing auditors and conducting other routine business.

The Official History of Blue Sky Mines

Important decisions have been taken, as usual, around the billiard table at the Croesus Club or in Pierpont's box at Royal Ascot. But Pierpont cannot remember any occasion, not even the dinner at Maxim's where we had to float a new company to pay the wine bill, that might have passed Henry Bosch's definition of a board meeting.

Nobody will ever know, because Penwiper has been forging board minutes regularly for the past decade. Indeed, the Blue Sky minutes have reached such a refined height of inventiveness that Penwiper is going to ask the Arts Council for a fiction grant.

Blue Sky could have continued functioning in this vein indefinitely, but for Sir Mark Time finally realising that it had been a long time between board meetings, putting the company in breach of everything that is fine and noble in the Companies Code 1981.

'You chaps must have forgotten,' he huffed. 'Just as well I'm on the ball, eh?' Which explains why we were gathered in the Blue Sky boardroom on a bright morning in late January.

Pierpont had the stopper out of the Macallan decanter and was pouring an aperitif for Spender, the accountant.

When Pierpont said that a quorum of directors was sober he was not including Bottle, the geologist, who had just flown in from Perth on the Red Eye Special. He had been imbibing alcohol continuously since the previous morning, when he had been negotiating options over gold claims in the Ironclad Hotel at Marble Bar.

Consequently, while the corporeal Bottle was with us, his spirit was still buying claims somewhere north of Nullagine. 'No more than ten thoushan' dollarsh,' he kept muttering. 'Mush be a good addressh . . .'

Sir Mark, in accordance with custom, was sitting at the head of the table in a catatonic trance.

It occurred to Pierpont that if the investing public could have glimpsed Sir Mark sitting there with his mental equipment apparently parked in cold storage for the summer, while Bottle babbled, Spender and Pierpont lowered the decanter, and Penwiper brought the last forgery up to date, the market would have been thick with sell orders.

Sir Mark blinked heavily, like one awaking from a deep sleep. 'I declare this meeting of Blue Sky Mines open,' he read painfully.

'Item one on the agenda is to approve the minutes of the last meeting.'

He paused, then shook his head like a spaniel coming out of a duck pond. 'Funny,' he remarked, 'I don't recall us having a meeting on Christmas Eve.'

'I sent the notification as usual, sir,' lied Penwiper. 'Australia Post is getting very slack these days.'

Sir Mark, who has never forgotten a balaclava which was lost in the post to him during the Dardanelles campaign, accepted this slander on the public service at its face value and took the minutes as read.

This brought us to the only other business of the morning, which was the float of Last Card Gold Mining No Liability.

Until now, the Last Card mine has been wholly owned by Blue Sky. Now the public is being offered 40 per cent of this existing gold mine for $4 million, the whole mine having recently been valued at $10 million by a visiting Canadian geologist who actually got within 500 kilometres of the mine while passing through the Ironclad with Bottle.

Bottle was under strict instructions to allow our visitor no closer to the mine, but to get his endorsement of a valuation which Bottle had already written. It took two hogsheads of Swan and half a flagon of muscat before the Canadian signed the report. The document is legal, having been witnessed by a barmaid, two drunks and – as far as we can judge – a cattle dog.

With the Canadian safely back in the wilds of Ontario wondering what happened to his liver, Blue Sky has sold 40 per cent of the mine to Last Card Gold Mining NL for $4 million.

Capital of the new company will be 25 million 50c shares paid to 20c each. These will be issued to the public, raising $5 million. Of this, $4 million goes to Blue Sky and $500,000 to Leo Liability the sharebroker for formation and underwriting expenses.

Normally no stockbroking firm would touch Blue Sky with a barge pole, but the public is so hungry for scrip at present that brokers will cheerfully underwrite anything.

This suits Blue Sky, because our corporate philosophy is to sell the Last Card mine in good times and buy it back in bad. Depending upon the fashions of the market, it has at times been a tantalite mine, an antimony mine, a tungsten mine and – if you go back far enough – a nickel mine. Any impoverished student who has ever tied a shilling to a piece of string so that it could be reused indefinitely in an English gas meter will grasp the principle.

How will we get it back? The finest print in the prospectus discloses an irrevocable agreement under which Last Card Gold Mining has undertaken to spend $1 million on development of the mine, and after that all development costs are to be shared 60/40 with Blue Sky.

But as Blue Sky and Leo Liability have already ripped $4.5 million of the $5 million out of Last Card Gold Mining, it will have to borrow to fulfil its commitment.

Who will lend it the money? Blue Sky, of course, under a first, floating debenture so comprehensive that it will cover every asset of Last Card Gold Mining down to the geologists' empty six-packs.

So unless they find gold in the mine, which is about equal to their chance of finding an inland sea, Last Card Gold Mining will default and Blue Sky will repossess everything including its 40 per cent stake.

The only details we had given Sir Mark were those concerning the float. After reading them, he turned to Bottle and asked: 'Four million dollars seems a lot for 40 per cent of Last Card. What do you think its real value is?'

'Ten thoushan' dollars ...' frothed Bottle, sliding gently under the board table.

'Well that seems a good deal, so let's do it!' exclaimed Sir Mark. He beamed around the board jovially. 'Jolly lucky I called this meeting, eh?'

IN ON THE MEZZANINE FLOOR

The first 10 minutes of the board meeting of Blue Sky Mines was a study in still life. Rembrandt would have liked to paint it.

Bottle and Pierpont were grouped around the decanter, taking long, appreciative draughts of Glendronach. Penwiper was forging the minutes of the last meeting. Spender the accountant was indulging in mental arithmetic.

This monastic silence was broken only by the faint grinding noise which indicated that the thinking processes of our chairman, Sir Mark Time, were in motion. He was staring at the agenda like a small bird hypnotised by a python.

The Boom Years

We thought for a while he may have lapsed into hibernation, but then he spoke.

'I don't seem to understand this,' he said. 'The only item on the agenda is to retrospectively approve a transaction in the shares of some company called Scylla Mining NL? Has anyone heard of it? And I am adamant that we should *never* be asked to approve of things retrospectively.'

Silence resumed as the other directors adopted an air of studied nonchalance. Pierpont slowly polished the crystal decanter stopper with loving care. Bottle could have been contemplating infinity. Penwiper studiously forged Sir Mark's signature on a blank cheque.

Spender lit a casual cigarette and said: 'I think you'll like this bit of retrospectivity, Sir Mark. Scylla's a new float that came on at $2. We bought a few on the recommendation of Leo Liability, the sharebroker. They went as high as $6 and we averaged $5 on the way out and still hold a parcel representing about 1 per cent of the company.'

'Smart work!' beamed Sir Mark. 'But are the shares still coming down?'

The Official History of Blue Sky Mines

'They may rise a little further,' said Spender. 'But Leo, who underwrote the float, thinks there may be some big selling orders in the wings as stags get out.'

'Very decent of him to let us know,' Sir Mark beamed again. 'If there were more brokers like Leo the world would be a finer place. Well, we all approve, don't we?'

And so we collected our attendance cheques and adjourned to the Croesus Club for lunch, Sir Mark being unaware that the tip of a financial iceberg had just floated past his consciousness.

If he had looked at the information memorandum of Scylla Mining he might have gleaned a little more of the story. Scylla's original capital consisted of three shares held by Bottle, Spender and Pierpont.

Scylla's main asset is the Charybdis gold mine in Western Australia. Or at least we call it a mine, but in fact it is a barren quartz reef, as white and hungry as a shark's tooth.

An el cheapo exploration program has so far yielded highly promising grades over a wide area, thanks to a sustained salting effort by Bottle, who has been dissolving small traces of gold in aqua regia and injecting them into the geologists' sample bags. In the process Bottle has used so many hypodermics that the Nullagine pharmacist is now firmly convinced he has graduated from Emu Bitter to heroin. Bottle has therefore achieved the not inconsiderable feat of lowering his reputation on the goldfields even further.

Armed with these results indicating a large, low-grade goldfield, Scylla's board commissioned a bored geologist to make a valuation of Charybdis. After an epic drinking bout with Bottle in the Palace Hotel (which ran it dry of both Bollinger and Emu Bitter), the geologist was persuaded to sign the valuation without actually visiting the reef.

The report valued Charybdis at $50 million and in accordance with standard accounting practice, the amount was credited to Scylla's asset revaluation reserve.

From this reserve, Scylla's directors granted themselves a bonus issue of 12 million $1 shares. Then after waiting a couple of months we had the float, in which another four million shares were offered to the public at a premium of 50c.

The capital structure of Scylla therefore looked like this:

The Boom Years

Holders	$
Original directors	3
Bonus issue to directors	12,000,000
Taken by public (4m. @ $1.50)	6,000,000
Total	18,000,003

Spender, Bottle and Pierpont therefore control three-quarters of Scylla, which now contains $6 million of public money, at no expense to ourselves except for a few thousand dollars spent on what we laughingly label exploration.

Actually the company does not have $6 million, because formation expenses took $800,000, including $600,000 to Leo Liability in underwriting commission. Of this, $400,000 went back to Bottle, Pierpont and Spender because we sub-underwrote the float.

By modern standards, Scylla is a nice, tight float with only 16 million shares issued and a mere four million of them in the hands of the public. And the net tangible asset backing (the geo's $50 million valuation, remember) is more than $3 a share. We made sure Scylla enjoyed a premium on listing by having Blue Sky push the price up.

Blue Sky bought a few hundred thousand shares from stags and baled out at a good profit. Now the directors have begun selling. If we had issued ourselves shares at the time of the float, they would be classed as vendor shares and we could not sell them for a year. As the bonus shares were an issue before listing they are not vendor shares and are under no restriction from being sold. Leo is unloading three million of our shares in digestible parcels at $6 and we don't mind if he sells the market gently down to $3. Considering we gave ourselves the shares for nothing, it's still a handsome profit.

We will still hold nine of the 16 million shares and hence control what happens to the $5.2 million cash.

Exactly how we will rob the investors of this we have not yet decided. The most obvious way would be to sell Scylla another mine of ours for $5 million.

The last thing that will happen, needless to say, is that the money will be spent on exploration.

This type of deal, where the promoters dodge vendor restrictions by making an issue to themselves before listing, is called 'mezzanine financing'.

Market speculators used to like to get in on the ground floor. We've found it's more profitable on the mezzanine.

A FEW GENERALLY ACCEPTED PRINCIPLES

For once, Blue Sky Mines No Liability has not had to commit perjury in announcing its annual results. Generally accepted accounting principles, stretched within the tolerable limits, have sufficed for us to produce as cosmetic a result as we could have desired. The directors, who normally contemplate seeing Paraguay about this time of year, have not even bothered to check whether their passports are still current.

Our results were put together a few days ago at Blue Sky's boardroom. Blue Sky has modernised its boardroom these days, notably by the addition of a loudspeaker giving share quotes and announcements made on the floor of the stock exchange. As speculative trading is the main activity of the directors, this was felt to be an essential aid, and so it would be if we could and some way of turning it off. As it is, the speaker crackles night and day and if Blue Sky board meetings were held more frequently — say, twice a year — we would be at risk of industrial deafness.

The other day the boardroom contained only Pierpont and Spender the accountant, who together comprise a quorum of the Blue Sky board (a fact carefully hidden from shareholders behind a shroud of legalese in the articles of association under 364AA(ix)(d) as amended in 1975).

Anyone stumbling upon us could have told instantly that it was a real director's meeting, as opposed to a formal one, because (a) our chairman, Sir Mark Time, was absent; (b) the minute books were off the table; and (c) the paper shredder was switched on and ready for action.

The loudspeaker crackled:

The Boom Years

'Ariadne Corp has sold 19.9 per cent of Renouf Corp to Joe's Milk Bar, Dunedin, for $450 million. The sale will realise a profit of $800 million to Adriadne.'

'Can't we turn that damned thing off?' grumbled Pierpont.

'Have another Bollinger,' advised Spender. 'We have to concentrate on the numbers.'

They were pretty simple in cash terms. In the year to June 30, Blue Sky's income had been $1,000 in interest from a small deposit. Expenses had totalled $1 million, comprising $10,000 on repair and maintenance of the company's only asset, the Last Card scheelite deposit, $40,000 in administration (mainly the salary of our secretary Penwiper) and $950,000 charged by directors in fees and overseas trips.

Pierpont jotted the numbers down:

Cash received	$1,000
Expenditure	$1,000,000
Loss	$999,000

Your average ignoramus would think Blue Sky had made a loss, but he would be reckoning without the glories of modern accounting. In today's accounting, a company does not have to receive money to have income and cash it has spent is an asset.

The Last Card mine has several hundred tonnes of ore at grass, which is a technical geological term for a big heap of mouldering dirt covered by weeds. As the value of tungsten on world markets is higher than the value attributed by Blue Sky to the tungsten in its stockpile, directors have revalued the stockpiles worth by $2 million.

Back in the dark days of accountancy, Blue Sky would have had to sell this ore before it could claim a profit.

But times have moved on. Modern companies such as Robt Jones in New Zealand revalue their buildings and claim the revaluation as a profit. So, until last year apparently, did Industrial Equity Ltd with its share portfolio. This has brought the modern discovery that a company no longer has to sell something to make a profit.

Spender jotted down Blue Sky's income as $2,000,000.

The loudspeaker crackled again: 'Adriadne Corp has sold 72.8 per cent of Renouf Corp to Martha's Fast Fish and Chips, Christchurch, for $3.7 billion, of which $10.8 billion is profit.'

Nor were Blue Sky's expenses actually costs. Owing to the tiresome practice by airlines of demanding money before lift-off, we did actually have to pay the directors' travel bills. But modern accountancy also allows a company to capitalise development costs.

The concept here is that where any project is still being brought to fruition, costs incurred in its development should be recognised as contributing to the worth of the asset and hence capitalised. This technique has the double beauty of removing expenses from the profit and loss account while writing up the values on the assets side of the balance sheet.

The repair and maintenance cost was capitalised immediately on these grounds. The directors' overseas travel was agreed (by Pierpont and Spender) to be essential market research and development.

If we want to cite a precedent on this one we might claim ACI, which in its 1975 results claimed 'pre-production expenses' of $5.6 million as an intangible asset, including $18,000 in directors' emoluments. Considering the pre-production expenses related to Pacific Can Ltd, which turned out to be one of ACI's big blunders of the era, our conscience is relaxed about using the same accounting technique on Last Card.

As a token, we left administration in as an expense. Having capitalised $960,000 worth of expenditure – a good morning's work – we cracked a Bollinger. The sums now read:

Revenue	$2,001,000
Expenses	$40,000
Profit	$1,961,000

And it's legal. We headed for the Croesus Club, determined to spend Blue Sky's hard-won profits before they should stray into the hands of undeserving shareholders.

As we left, the loudspeaker crackled again:

'Ariadne Corp Ltd has sold 124 per cent of Renouf Corp to Bill's Garage, Wanganui, for one thousand million billion zillion dollars, of which $NZ7.24 was cash. Mr Bruce Judge has become a director of Marth's Fast Fish and Chips, Christchurch, and Mrs Judge has secured the lamington concession at Joe's Milk Bar for $173 million.'

The Boom Years

TECHNICAL BRIEF 3

HOW TO RUN A MINING COMPANY

With a gold and diamond boom off and running since January, there has been a disturbing rise in the number of small speculative companies which have discovered real live mines. What is more, some of them will actually be mined.

In these circumstances, Pierpont believes he should waste no time in reassuring shareholders of Blue Sky Mines that there is absolutely no danger of their company finding, let alone operating, a real mine. At Blue Sky we believe that ore deposits are for pegging and trading and attracting favourable publicity at the right time. Blue Sky mines only the share market and will continue to do so.

Judging by the number of successful insider trading prosecutions so far in Australia's history, this seems a perfectly safe occupation and considerably more rewarding than trudging through the hot, weary bush and the even drearier ritual of consulting with Aborigines and greenies and governments who know even less about mining than we do.

But having observed a number of mining mishaps from the safe vantage point of the gin cupboard, Pierpont has assembled the following manual for junior explorers who are rash enough to actually dig holes in the ground.

1. Location
The first rule with any mine is to make sure it's in the right place. The geologists of Australia have been very careless over the years about where they found mines. Remote, arid places such as Telfer, Mount Isa and Roxby Downs. Pierpont's ideal location is the Three Mile in Western Australia. As Metana's Graeme ('Champ') Hutton said: 'It's perfect, Pierpont. On the highway and three miles from the pub.' Now that's what Pierpont calls a great mine location.

2. The orebody
For want of any alternative, initial mining should be based on the hypothesis that the orebody is the size and grade which the geologist calculated in the reserve statement. This has never yet been known to be accurate, but until you get down there you can't

work it out for yourself. The reserve statement for Mount Percy, for example, gave a gold content estimate that turned out to be double the eventual mine grade. And much the same can be said for the initial 3.56 per cent nickel grade announced by the old Poseidon mine at Windarra.

The Dittmer mine in Queensland, reopened by Buddha Gold in 1980, had an assay laboratory on site that reported grades averaging 5.4 grams to the tonne. After three months spent losing money mining Dittmer, the company discovered the smelter grades on the same ore showed it was 2.7 grams – exactly half.

3. Aliens

Watch out for UFOs. So many of our gold mines have disappeared that the only logical explanation is that they must have been stolen by aliens. To take one example, Lightning Ridge in 1983 bought the Clermont gold mine in Queensland on the basis of 'highly encouraging reports from consultants, and evaluations of earlier work and studies on the area' which showed 960,000 cubic metres of 'proven mineable alluvial material' at an average grade of 0.6 grams.

The company commissioned a plant, put through 40,000 cubic metres and discovered that gold returns were 'significantly below the geological grade estimates' and put the mine on care and maintenance. Clermont had been a mine for just eight weeks. When Lightning Ridge repanned the previous test sites it found the average grade was below 0.2 grams. So what happened to 0.6? Obviously aliens stole it.

This theory is supported by the experience of Aurex Alluvials, which raised $2.8 million when it floated in September 1983 on the Stawell River prospect, where the directors said they had a reasonable expectation that reserves would be proven 'sufficient in volume and grade to justify a mining operation'. Aurex shovelled only 157 cubic metres through the plant before relinquishing the prospect. Aliens again.

4. Public Relations

Hiring a creative PR firm will do more for your share price than a carbon-in-pulp plant. The classic case is Murumba Minerals, one of the rather large number of companies that in 1972 had recently suffered the traumatic experience of being run by Alexander Barton.

Murumba was taken over by a WA entrepreneur, whose first action was to hire a public relations company. In a letter to the PR firm, he said: 'Needless to say, I envisage a strong PR campaign for Murumba as far as the financial press is concerned. I would suggest that this involves far more than the circulation of press releases and requires a detailed study of shareholders' emotive needs during the next 18 months or so.

A flash of true insight. Mining is not about ore grades or metallurgy. It's about satisfying investors' emotive needs. That's very important to remember.

5. Waste Rock
It's not. It's ore at grass.

6. Dewatering
Never pump out an old mine unless you are absolutely sure you know what's below the water. You were probably sold the mine with a story about the old-timers pulling out rich ore until they hit the water table and then having to retreat because the old pumps couldn't handle it.

It might be true, but the old-timers were pretty smart and sometimes they quit simply because the good ore ran out.

Better to leave the mine full to the brim and sell it to the next wood duck.

PIERPONT'S
TAXPAYERS START HERE
HIRE TAX ACCOUNTANT
SET UP HONG KONG TRUST
BUY SHARES FOR DIVIDEND IMPUTATION
BLUE SKY MINES
YOUR COMPANY CAR TAKEN BACK
NEGATIVE GEAR PROPERTY
FOUNDATIONS SINK
WHITE ANTS ANOTHER $5,000
INHERIT UNCLE'S ESTATE GO STRAIGHT TO PAUL KEATING
SPEND ANOTHER $10,000
WALK FOR REST OF GAME
BUY FARM
PERFECT TAXPAYER PREPARES FOR MARTYRDOM
SPEND $100,000 ON IMPROVEMENTS
READ 26AAA FALL ASLEEP
WAKE TO FIND RE-ASSESSMENT IN MAIL
O.H.M.S.
PENALTY-PAY $20,000 OR GO STRAIGHT TO PAUL KEATING
LOSE RECEIPTS RETURN TO START
DROUGHT
BUY BONDS
INTEREST RATES RISE - BONDS FALL
TAX SHELTER
COWS DIE
TWO YEARS LATER-GOOD SEASON-PROFIT EXPECTED
ARMY TAKES OVER PROPERTY
BOTTOM OF THE HARBOUR

TAX GUIDE
FILM SCHEME SAVE $1,000 TAX LOSE $20,000 INVESTMENT
INVEST IN GOLD MINES
TWO DAYS LATE LODGING RETURN FINED $10,000
SHARE MARKET COLLAPSES NO DIVIDEND
SELL PROPERTY-GAINS TAXED-EXPENSES DISALLOWED
TAXMAN SAYS CALLS NOT DEDUCTIBLE
VANCOUVER DIPLOMATIC POST
HONG KONG GOES COMMUNIST - THINK ABOUT SUICIDE
LUNCH WITH THE A.T.O. PRETEND TO ENJOY BREAD AND WATER
GOLD TAXED
GET LITERARY GRANT
YOUR ACCOUNTANT GAOLED RETURN TO START
INVEST IN HIGH-TECH
TAKE WIFE ON BUSINESS TRIP
APPLY FOR JOB ON BICENTENNIAL AUTHORITY
FREQUENT FLYER POINTS TAXED
GET FREE OVERSEAS FLIGHT
MOVE TO BALMAIN
JOIN A POLITICAL PARTY
SOAP
PROMISES
BECOME AN M.P.
TAX FREE INCOME
$

4

AFTER THE GREAT CRASH

~

*W*estern Civilisation As We Know It died on Black Tuesday: October 20, 1987. The Australian share market opened 25 per cent down on the buyer quotes. Amongst more or less respectable stocks, that is. There was no market at all in speculatives such as Blue Sky. Some of the cowboys kept soldiering on for a while after October 20, notably Warwick Fairfax in his takeover of the family newspaper company. (He then fought a court case with Laurie Connell's Rothwells and managed to save $73 million of the promised fee, but only after washing a lot of dirty linen in public.)

The all ordinaries bottomed in March 1988 under 1300 — more than 1000 points down in six months. It managed to recover 300 points by the mid-1989, but it was crucified by Treasurer Paul Keating pushing interest rates to the highest sustained levels seen in modern Australia. Over the same period the gold price slid from $US470 to $US370.

Corporate honesty was maintained under the stern vigilance of the NCSC.

JUST A BIT TOO MUCH CAPITAL

Thank you for asking but no, the Great Crash did not wipe out Blue Sky Mines No Liability. Blue Sky's investment portfolio emerged showing a few shell holes, but as we had previously exploited the bull market to the hilt with a few equity raisings, Blue Sky was indecently opulent as November 1987 dawned.

When the share market was soaring earlier this year, investors became so unselective that Blue Sky's price rose despite the activities of its directors. We immediately mined the market (we don't really mine anything else) with a 1-for-7 premium issue, followed by a 1-for-10 at par. The unprecedentedly high price also prompted long-suffering holders of several million old options to convert.

At one point the money was rolling into Blue Sky faster than the directors could think of new ways to rob the company, with the result that we still have some cash on hand. How the directors can remove this from Blue Sky's coffers is a problem and that – not the Great Crash – is the reason our brows are furrowed these days.

Indeed we are rather grateful for the Great Crash because all the scribes were so excited about covering Black Tuesday that they failed to notice little announcements such as the one put out by Blue Sky amending the notice of annual meeting to add a resolution increasing authorised capital.

It would take a very astute investor to couple this with the fact that Blue Sky has not yet released its annual report. Blue Sky decided its profit – after stretching generally accepted accounting principles to their rubbery limit – just before October 20. At that point we thought we could produce the annual report within a few days, but we struck a small unforeseen snag.

Pierpont became aware of this only when he was summoned to an emergency meeting of the board. Spender and Bottle were present but not our chairman Sir Mark Time.

'What's the trouble?' Pierpont grumped querulously. 'I thought we'd straightened out the profit.'

'That isn't the problem,' replied Spender.

'Then what is?'

'We don't know our issued capital.'

The Official History of Blue Sky Mines

It took some time for this to sink in. Then Pierpont reached for the decanter and poured himself a long, stiff Macallan as Penwiper and Spender explained what had happened.

There had been heavy turnover in Blue Sky shares during the year. Our share register had fallen behind and so had the brokers' back offices. Applications for rights issues had been sent to people who had sold their stock and they had applied successfully for the new shares. This meant that we had sometimes supplied rights to both the buyer and seller of the same share.

Option holders who had converted had applied for and received shares even though they had converted after the entitlement date. Where the option buyer had sold again quickly he had sometimes received undeserved rights to the issue also. And thanks to a computer breakdown the share registry – run by Spender's brother-in-law – had lost count of the certificates it had issued.

The result of this monumental foul-up, which is still unreconciled in brokers' back rooms around the country, is that nobody knows how many shares Blue Sky has on issue. We can estimate it to the nearest million, but anything more specific is too hard. As Pierpont drained his second Macallan and wondered what Henry Bosch would say about all this, Penwiper added: 'There's one more problem, sir.'

Pierpont poured himself another stiff one before asking: 'Yes?'

'Whatever our issued capital is, sir, it must exceed our authorised capital. We issued a lot of options and a lot of old ones got converted that we never expected and we sort of lost count. We . . . er . . . seem to have been issuing shares illegally, sir.'

Pierpont thought back. In the excitement of mining the market, nobody had thought to check the authorised capital, which limits the number of shares a company can issue. When the old options came into the money and the punters converted, we must have gone well over.

So our annual accounts are going to show issued capital at just below the authorised level. With any luck this black lie will go undetected, while we whip the increase in authorised capital through as a special motion at the annual meeting. Afterwards we will announce a share placement large enough to take us to our best guess of what the issued capital actually is.

We would sack Spender's brother-in-law as well, but he seems to be performing at about par for an Australian share registry these days.

BLUE SKY LAYS ANOTHER SMOKESCREEN

Sir Mark Time, chairman of Blue Sky Mines No Liability and professional dunderhead, leaned forward on the board table to peer through the cigar smoke.

'Sorry if I'm a bit slow calling the meeting to order today,' he apologised. 'The trouble is, I can't see whether we've got a quorum or not.'

It occurred to Pierpont, puffing contentedly on his fourth Cohina, that the air was becoming a trifle thick. On his right, Bottle the geologist was down to the stub of his third Partagas, while Spender the accountant, who on principle refuses to buy Cuban produce, was sucking at a tightly packed corona from Jamaica. Even Sir Mark had just lit a Carl Upmann, making the whole scene reminiscent of the Royal Navy laying smokescreens at the Battle of Jutland.

At the end of the table, Penwiper – our poor but dishonest secretary – crushed a Benson & Hedges in his ashtray and said: 'They must all be here, Sir Mark. I counted them on the way in and nobody has left.'

'Well, the only door is at your end, so let me know if you see any of them leave,' Sir Mark instructed.

Then, turning to Spender, he said: 'The only item on the agenda is the takeover of Gung Ho Gold Mines No Liability. Why does that name seem familiar?'

Spender, his cheeks hollow from the effort of drawing smoke through a corona that had obviously been rolled by a very firm virgin, said: 'Perhaps the name is familiar because it is an associated company. Blue Sky floated it a year ago when the gold boom was running. As a declaration of interest I should point out that Pierpont, Bottle and myself were vendors.'

All quite true, for once. The market had been running so hot at the end of 1986 that even Blue Sky shares were attracting a premium on the specious grounds that it was a speculative veteran. So it put a few gold claims together, Bottle having first carefully inspected them

The Official History of Blue Sky Mines

to ensure there was no risk of any actual gold being discovered, and put them into a prospectus in return for four million of the 10 million fully paid 50c shares.

Bottle, Pierpont and Spender had also put same pieces of West Australian scrubland into Gung Ho in return for half a million vendor shares and $1 million cash. After a few expenses, Gung Ho therefore had 10 million shares and a little over $2 million cash.

Then two significant recent events occurred. First, after Black Tuesday the shares had fallen to 8c, although their cash backing was still slightly over 20c. Second, the vendor shares, which were issued with a one-year restriction, were now free to be sold.

So Blue Sky is making a takeover bid at 12c. Pierpont, Bottle and Spender, who had already made their profit at the front end, by ripping $1 million out of the public float, will receive another $60,000, which is at least 50 per cent better than they would do trying to sell large blocks of Gung Ho on market.

Blue Sky will outlay $720,000 buying the stock it does not already own in Gung Ho and receive $2 million cash plus some gold claims which will be useful for another prospectus one day. That is, after all, the whole technique for mining the market. Sell the public overpriced assets in bull markets and buy them back at less than asset backing in bear markets.

Meanwhile the cash in Blue Sky's kitty will be swollen by a net $1.3 million. Pierpont and his fellow thieves on the board do not yet know exactly how we will divert that cash to ourselves, but rest assured we will. We have not bothered to mention this to Sir Mark because his brain is capable of holding only one thought at a time and we do not wish to overstrain it.

Which is why we are smoking big cigars despite the collapsing speculative market.

'Like to try one of mine?' Pierpont asked Spender.

'Do you mind?' said Spender.

'Delighted,' replied Pierpont.

The takeover was approved and, there being no other business, the meeting adjourned.

A BIT SHORT OF BLUE SKY

The Glendronach decanter had made two circuits of the board table of Blue Sky Mines No Liability before the chairman, that old dunderhead Sir Mark Time, had finished reading the monthly accounts. The rest of the directors were nonchalant, but a keen observer might have detected a slightly furtive air about them.

Luckily Sir Mark has never been a keen observer. Indeed that is the old drone's sole qualification for being chairman of Blue Sky.

'I must say you chaps are handling the crisis frightfully well,' he said at last. 'We seem to have plenty of cash in the bank and our big exploration program has been husbanded rather well.'

Bottle the geologist almost blushed, a phenomenon that would have created history in his profession. Pierpont has known many a geo in his decades on the battlefields of finance and can testify that the mantle of shame has been somehow left out of their metabolism.

'We've been keeping exploration on the Great Pyrite mine to a minimum during the boom because the contractors have been overcharging,' he extemporised. In truth, of course, Sir Mark is the only director who does not realise that it is high policy of Blue Sky never to commit mining.

Mining in any form is dirty, dangerous, explosive and the shareholders never thank you for undertaking it. The shareholders' sole interest is the price they can get for their shares, so Blue Sky has taken this to its logical conclusion by mining the share market instead of the ground. The lack of activity at our various mine sites is such that at any day now we expect to win an award from the Australian Conservation Foundation.

'You know,' Sir Mark mused, 'Considering how thriftily we've handled Blue Sky's fortunes, I'm surprised the share price has fallen so far. If I recall rightly, it hit $2 at the height of the boom, but it started sliding even before Black Tuesday and now it's down to 15 cents. The selling seems to have been particularly heavy in London.'

Spender the accountant took the cue. 'The markets have simply panicked,' he explained. 'Many small stocks such as Blue Sky are now selling below asset backing. However, Leo Liability the stockbroker has set up a London office now and should be able to explain the merits of Blue Sky to the markets there.'

'Hmmph!' snorted Sir Mark. 'His firm seems to be doing most of the selling.'

Perhaps it was the Glendronach, but Sir Mark was showing dangerous signs of sentience this morning. The truth was that Spender, Bottle and Pierpont had, through an untraceable chain of overseas nominee companies, been selling Blue Sky short. In 1986 we had been the vendors of Great Pyrite, which contains less gold than the average wedding ring, and taken vendor stock which had been in escrow for a year. We had sold this on market about a month before it was due to come out of escrow and had since delivered it to Leo's London office, which been set up largely to play this kind of game.

Then, judging the market was turning, we began selling Blue Sky short. Blue Sky is not one of the prescribed stocks that can be shorted in Australia, but you can short anything in London. We sold nearly two million shares, driving the price down to present levels. We stand to average a profit of around $1 per share if we can cover existing market levels.

After the Great Crash

But if we buy Blue Sky back on the present thin market there is grave danger that we will put the price up.

'I must admit, however, that Leo seems to be doing some good for us,' Sir Mark conceded, looking at the last item on the agenda. 'He has managed to make a placement of nearly two million shares at 20c. That's pretty good going in this market. And raises enough money for a couple of years' exploration at this rate, eh?'

No prizes for guessing who will pick up the placement. We use the placement to cover the short sales. As long as we retain board control we can play this game until infinity. One of these days Blue Sky may well make a big placement at half a cent.

The trick is to retain board control. Next time we might do it by having a stiff rights issue underwritten by Leo. We could short the stock, then announce something like a one-for-one at 10c. Shareholders would dump the shares rather than pick up the issue and we could probably cover at 1c.

With any luck, as they never know what bits of paper they're holding in London, we could even cover it with the shortfall from the issue, while simultaneously regaining control at low prices.

(This technique might have been pioneered by others in London, so Pierpont will be careful not to take credit from the rightful inventors.)

One needs a co-operative broking house for this sort of ploy, but Leo is renowned for his co-operativeness. Indeed, it is the usual cause of his appearances before the stock exchange disciplinary committee.

'Leo's really doing excellent work, Sir Mark,' Pierpont observed. 'I thought you were being a bit harsh on him a minute ago.'

'Sorry if I was,' Sir Mark apologised. 'I suppose the chap is bound to execute orders from his clients. But I must say I find it surprising that he should have one batch of clients who are big sellers and another batch who are big buyers.'

'That's a great recommendation for him,' said Pierpont. 'It just shows how strong the Chinese Walls must be at Leo's firm. Now if that's all for today, we've just got time for an aperitif before a spot of lunch at the Croesus Club.'

KEEPING IT UNDERGROUND

Truth to tell, Pierpont was by no means fully alert when Blue Sky Mines held its board meeting this week. He had attended Penfolds Great Wine Dinner the night before.

The warm-up had been a little tasting of a dozen wines, including the 1976 and 1980 St Henris, and Mrs Pierpont had become upset at the sight of some of the more amateur tasters spitting the wine into ice buckets.

'How ghastly!,' she exclaimed.

'Quite right, m'dear,' Pierpont agreed, and dutifully swallowed every glass so as not to offend. By the time he had worked through to dessert (almond tuille filled with fresh strawberry yoghurt and perfumed with Grand Marnier) your correspondent was feeling absolutely no pain.

That arrived next morning, when Pierpont was grappling with a steaming beaker of Andronicus and hoping that life would soon return to his ageing frame. Even so, he was in better shape than Sir Mark Time, who was clutching the agenda with no sign of cognition.

'I know we agreed to have another share issue,' he said plaintively. 'But this one seems rather high. Why are we having a 1-for-1 at 20c when the shares are only 25c on market?'

Pierpont, still being incapable of coherent speech, stayed silent. So did Penwiper, who usually speaks only when spoken to at board meetings. Today he was sitting at the end of the table, working diligently on his copperplate. Penwiper is studying for his Advanced Forgery Certificate and will sit for his exam in Promissory Notes III next Monday.

Spender the accountant was the only other board member present (Bottle being absent on a field trip to Kalgoorlie) so he shouldered the burden of the reply.

'Blue Sky is in a strong expansionary phase at present exploring our new gold prospect at Bull-Ant Bore, and we cannot afford to be deflected by the vagaries of the share market,' he said. 'And if our shareholders have faith I am sure they will stand by us.'

By and large, all in all, and generally speaking, this was a lie. The directors already hold 60 per cent of Blue Sky and the aim of the issue is to squeeze out as many minority shareholders as we can because Bull-Ant is looking promising. That is why Bottle went west.

This is also why Bottle, Spender and Pierpont have underwritten the issue. We intend to mop up the shortfall, release the good news on Bull-Ant Bore, then sell on a rising market. We have masked our intentions by having the issue sub-underwritten.

Sir Mark's brow was furrowed as he exercised his grey cells – or such of them as were not extinct. 'That may be all well and good,' he snorted. 'But I don't like the sub-underwriter. Didn't we have a nasty experience with him last time?'

'Oh, no, Sir Mark. That was just a clerical error,' Spender interposed quickly.

It was nothing of the sort. When we made the previous issue the shares were 70c on market and Blue Sky pitched the issue price at 50c. We gave the sub-underwriting to a London broker whom Pierpont will call Andy Capp. This was a mistake, because Andy – using the vast free zone of the London market – promptly shorted bundles of the stock down to 50c. Shareholders refused to subscribe to the issue, which suited Andy fine because he then covered his position with the shares he picked up in the sub-underwriting.

This time we have set a little trap. Andy has already begun shorting the stock and will certainly push it back to par of 20c. Then he will expect to pick up the shortfall to cover. At this point we will blandly tell him that the issue was fully subscribed.

Andy will know we are lying but will have no way of proving it. Nor will he be able to lodge a complaint or take any legal action without revealing his illegal shorting. To cover his position, he will have to buy back on market, which by that time the directors will have pushed to 40c. We will not only sell him all the real shortfall from the issue, but some of our own stock as well. The directors will make a profit, Andy will be punished and Blue Sky will have some money in the bank for once. A fairytale ending, in fact.

None of this, naturally, has been revealed to Sir Mark, who mumbled assent to the proposed issue. As he adjourned the meeting, Bottle lurched into the room, having just landed on the Red-Eye Special. He staggered up to Pierpont, blear-eyed and with the aroma of Palace Hotel whisky still rich upon him.

'There'sh gold at Bull-Ant,' he slurred excitedly. 'Half an ounsh a tonne. It'sh going to be a bonansha.' He dug into one pocket and pulled out a nugget the size of a golf ball. 'There'sh gold!' he repeated.

'No, there isn't,' hissed Pierpont, thankful for once that Sir Mark is a trifle deaf. 'How many times do we have to tell you that we can't find gold before the books close on the issue?'

'Shorry,' whispered Bottle, realising his mistake. 'But I got exkshited.'

'Think nothing of it,' said Pierpont, noting that Sir Mark was heading to the boardroom bar oblivious of the interference. 'Just go straight back to the West, drop that nugget back down a percussion hole and don't discover it again for a fortnight. Then we can really ramp the shares on Andy.'

DEAR DIARY ...

The late, great humorist Lennie Lower advised people who were tempted to make New Year resolutions to only make those which they would have no trouble keeping. Lennie, for instance, used to resolve not to drink out of horse troughs on Sundays.

Not for the first time in his long life, Pierpont is wishing he listened to such sage advice, because your correspondent is already having trouble with his own resolution. As the strains of Auld Lang Syne were dying at the Pierpont manse on New Year's Eve, Pierpont took a deep draught of Bollinger and a vow that henceforth he would keep a diary.

After the Great Crash

He was prodded into this resolution because the lower orders in Australia are getting out of hand. Back in the good old days a respectable financier such as Pierpont was rightly seen as a person whose repute was beyond question. But in this prying modern world, everyone from the Fitzgerald Inquiry in Queensland to the Australian Taxation Office has the right to summons Pierpont before a judge and ask him detailed questions about his private finances.

And Pierpont's memory being notoriously unreliable, your correspondent is bound to perjure himself in the first five minutes. An old lawyer once advised Pierpont that there were only six answers to give in the witness box:
1. **Yes.**
2. No.
3. I don't know.
4. I don't remember.
5. I don't understand the question.
6. Will you please repeat the question.

Pierpont spent a few days watching the Rothwells case recently while Warwick Fairfax was giving evidence. Your correspondent came away with the impression that Warwick's legal adviser had never heard of the first two answers, but had taken out a world monopoly on the sixth.

The Official History of Blue Sky Mines

What worried Pierpont most about the whole distasteful affair was the detail that your average QC expects the average businessman to remember of dates, meetings and conversations.

So in fear that one day your correspondent would be cowering in the witness box while some bully of a barrister kept asking: 'Where were you on the night of the 27th?', Pierpont resolved that in 1989 he would keep a diary. Pierpont maintained this resolve for the first two days of the year, sitting at his study desk and dutifully noting the receipt of dividends and his phone calls to brokers.

The real test came on Tuesday. Pierpont was sitting in the Jim Fisk Bar of the Croesus Club, having an aperitif or three, when Spender the accountant joined him and ordered our first Bollinger for the year. This being a historic event, Pierpont jotted down 'R.D. No. 1' on the noon line.

'The year has started on a high note,' Spender chuckled. 'We've found a buyer for the Grubsville shopping centre.'

Pierpont jotted down "year high buyer Grubsville centre" before the full import of the statement struck home. This shopping centre is a joint venture between Pierpont and Spender with a little real estate subsidiary of Blue Sky called Krakatoa Properties Ltd. We scoured the outskirts of the city for the cheapest large block available and found it in a reclaimed sewage farm at Grubsville, a modern slum suburb where only the severely deranged would want to live.

'Well it's nicely located on two main roads,' Pierpont recalled. 'But the problem has always been that the local residents can't afford to buy anything.'

'Yes,' replied Spender. 'We never got around to a demographic study of the neighbourhood.'

We never got around to much else either. We only bought because the land was 10 hectares and cheap. We bribed the local building surveyor, had it rezoned commercial and smuggled through a development application for a shopping centre. We built the centre before anyone could object, but also before the builder could indulge in such fripperies as soil testing. The result is that we now have a slapdash concrete monstrosity with sinking foundations.

In the grip of his new habit, Pierpont jotted down 'No demographic study. Sinking foundations', then paused for a refreshing draught of the R.D.'73 Extra Brut. All this literary activity was

After the Great Crash

beginning to fatigue your correspondent and he was wondering how professional writers ever find time to become alcoholics. Perhaps they drink with the left hand, because otherwise they must imbibe under handicap. Pierpont had barely got outside one glassful, but Spender was already ordering a second bottle.

'Who's the buyer?' asked Pierpont.

'The Banzai Property Trust,' whispered Spender. 'They're paying $20 million.'

Pierpont felt a gentle pang of compassion for Banzai, a new Japanese-backed outfit which had just begun investing in Australian real estate. Two or three more purchases like Grubsville and we would have avenged the fall of Singapore.

Pierpont scribbled 'Sold Banzai, $20m.' in his diary, an entry which became immediately soaked as his left hand spilled half a flute of Bollinger over the page. Pierpont mopped the diary down with a handkerchief and returned the glass to his dexter paw.

'In business these days, it's not what you're selling that's important, but what you seem to be selling,' Spender pontificated. 'In shopping centres, the buyers want high yields, so we have to show full occupancy at high rents.'

That had always been a problem at Grubsville, where nearly three-quarters of the shops had been standing empty.

'How did we fill the stores?' asked Pierpont.

'Phantom tenants,' replied Spender. 'I invented a dozen business names, recruited some of the scourings of the neighbourhood to stand behind counters and drew up rental contracts with them. Our company, Krakatoa, lends them the money, they subtract 10 per cent for themselves and pay us the rent. Banzai sees a fully tenanted shopping centre and buys.'

Pierpont's mind was moving more slowly than his right hand, which had jotted 'phantom tenants, fake contracts' before your correspondent realised what he was doing.

'How long will the tenants stay in place?' asked Pierpont.

'Until five minutes after settlement with Banzai,' grinned Spender, ordering a third.

Pierpont looked at his diary. It was covered with ungainly scribble, soaked in champagne and now contained enough evidence to send your correspondent to stone college until the Tricentennial. Pierpont tore out the incriminating page and with some difficulty managed to set it on fire in the ashtray and reduce it to charred pulp.

Then he looked at the diary again. 'Why?' (he could hear some bully of a barrister snarling) 'Why did you tear out the diary entry for January the 3rd?'

With a sigh, Pierpont leaned across the bar and dumped the rest of the diary into the barman's refuse bin.

'I've been wondering why you were cluttering yourself up with that thing,' said Spender. 'By the way, did you make any New Year's resolutions?'

WHEN I'M CALLING YOU

Having sat himself comfortably at the boardroom table Pierpont inhaled deeply, building up a half-inch of ash on his freshly-lit Davidoff. He took a long swallow of Glendronach from his tumbler, then poured himself another generous four fingers of malt.

Thus primed, he was in fighting shape for the current board meeting of Blue Sky Mines NL.

Your correspondent had discerned at a glance that it was a serious meeting, because the minute books were off the table and our chairman – that old drone Sir Mark Time – was not present.

Apart from Pierpont, the others at the table were his fellow directors – Spender, Bottle and Penwiper, who was diligently practis-

After the Great Crash

ing forgeries of Sir Mark's signature. This was therefore a working meeting as opposed to the formal ones in which Sir Mark is quickly glided through the agenda and persuaded to sign a blank page of the minute book in much the same way as a scientist might guide a blind mouse through a laboratory maze.

Pierpont took another snifter of Glendronach to sharpen his brain cells. It is always your correspondent's policy to keep his wits about him at such meetings to guard against the possibility, however remote, that we might transact some business that accidentally benefits the shareholders.

'I apologise for breaking into your Swiss holiday,' Spender began. 'But a recent move by one of our fellow explorers has set a precedent which Blue Sky might exploit.'

With that, Spender handed out copies of an announcement by Tuckanarra Minerals NL, which has made a three-for-two bonus issue to shareholders. The interesting aspect of this particular issue was that while Tuckanarra's existing shares were fully paid 50c par value, the bonus shares being issued had a nominal value of 40c and were paid only to 25c.

Now while Pierpont always enjoys a bonus, he has seen many a contributing share that was not so much a bonus as a penalty. Holders of partly paid shares are always apt to be smitten by calls at inopportune times. But in Tuckanarra's case this would appear a remote threat because it is a no liability company and holders can therefore sacrifice their shares if they do not wish to pay a call. Also, the largest shareholder in Tuckanarra when anyone last counted was Peter Briggs, and Pierpont somehow cannot conceive Peter paying large calls on shares.

Tuckanarra is doing a number of interesting things, such as exploring an exciting gold prospect south of Da Nang in Vietnam and making an issue of its fully paid and partly paid shares to take over another Peter Briggs company called New Australian Resources NL. This bid sounds as though it might be for hometown players only, so Pierpont will wish Peter well but not commit any of his cigar money to Tuckanarra or New Australian stock just yet.

Anyhow, now that a blue chip stock such as Tuckanarra has set the scene, Blue Sky's directors intend to follow suit in their own way. Holders of Blue Sky's 50c fully paid shares will soon be delighted to receive a five-for-one bonus issue of 25c paid shares. As Blue Sky's fully paid stock is only 22c at present, the theoretical value of the contributing shares is roughly zero but they are something for nothing for the shareholders.

Over the next few months, the directors will release a series of promising exploration announcements which should push the value of the fully paids to 40c and the contribs to 15c.

Then directors will make a 5c call for the alleged development of some alleged mine (don't ask Pierpont the name because it doesn't exist yet and indeed it will never exist as a mine in future).

Human psychology is such that most punters will pay 5c to protect something that is priced at 15c. Over the next five years, we could make five 5c calls and raise enough money to buy our own Swiss ski resort.

Young Penwiper spotted a flaw. 'But, sir!' he exclaimed to Spender. 'The directors will have to pay calls as well. You're surely not going to put your own money into Blue Sky?'

Pierpont quieted the lad's fears. 'There's no risk of that, son,' your correspondent said, ashing his Davidoff on the carpet. 'We will forfeit our contributing shares, then have a sale.'

Forfeited shares must by law be sold at public auction but can be sold for any price. Blue Sky's forfeited share auction will be held at midnight on Good Friday in the middle of a Kakadu swamp. It will be over in a flash and the parcel will be sold for a total of $1.

The buyers will, of course, be Spender, Bottle and Pierpont. Having gone through the legal necessity of a forfeited share auction, the shares will be credited as paid to the amount of the call and our equity in the company will be preserved.

'So all we need to do now is hold a formal board meeting and get Sir Mark to sign the minutes,' said Bottle.

'Er ... that won't be necessary,' said Penwiper, whose copperplate had been working overtime. 'He's already signed them.'

WHO KILLED ROUND ROBIN?

Thank heavens for Alan Bond and Christopher Skase. The pursuit of these two heroes of corporate Australia has taken up so much of the time of the banks, the NCSC and the Australian Stock Exchange that

After the Great Crash

nobody has yet noticed the failure of Blue Sky Mines (No Liability Except At Gunpoint) to lodge its profit statement or accounts for the year to June.

The board has struck an impasse that appears to be quite, totally, absolutely, insoluble. As Pierpont has explained before, Sir Mark Time's main qualification as chairman is that he is never likely to notice the campaign of rape, loot and pillage that the rest of us have been conducting for years against the shareholders.

One of the many things which Sir Mark does not know is that Blue Sky's profit and loss account was to have been boosted in the year to June by a round-robin conspiracy with another company named Rockbound Mining No Liability. The round-robin was to have worked as follows:

1. Blue Sky borrows $5 million from The Hungry Bank.
2. Blue Sky lends $5 million to Rockbound.
3. Rockbound offers $5 million for Blue Sky's Last Card scheelite deposit.
4. Blue Sky sells Last Card for $5 million, which represents $1 million profit and will bring us up to break-even for the year.

After balance date (i.e. 9 a.m. on July 1) the whole deal was to have been reversed, with Blue Sky buying back the mine, Rockbound repaying the loan and the $5 million plus a tad of interest being repaid to The Hungry Bank. Blue Sky and Rockbound have conspired in similar plots in previous years, but this time it came unglued.

On June 30, eight sinister figures gathered in a conference room at The Hungry Bank. Representing Blue Sky were Spender, Bottle, Pierpont and Penwiper, our poor but dishonest secretary. Representing Rockbound were its three directors, Swizzle, Diddle and Shaft.

Representing the bank was a so-called financial adviser named Hotfoot, who charges by the minute. Looking at the cunning, evil faces of his co-conspirators around the table, Pierpont was surprised that some innocent teller had not sounded the police alarm when we had walked in. But then, they're used to cunning, evil faces around The Hungry Bank.

As usual in a round-robin, everyone was to exchange cheques simultaneously. Blue Sky borrowed $5 million from The Hungry Bank – whose business would be halved if it did not finance book-fiddling exercises such as this. Hotfoot gave Spender a cheque and Penwiper minuted the transaction. Blue Sky loaned $5 million to Rockbound by Spender pushing a cheque of ours across the table to Swizzle. Again, Penwiper minuted the transaction.

Then Rockbound's three directors began a board meeting, with Swizzle keeping the minutes. The first item of business was to note receipt of Blue Sky's loan. The second item was to place the money on deposit with The Hungry Bank. Swizzle, Diddle and Shaft accordingly endorsed Blue Sky's cheque and pushed it along the table to Hotfoot, who gave Rockbound a receipt.

Then Swizzle scribbled quickly in the minute book and rose to his feet. 'My conscience will no longer permit me to take part in such blatant frauds upon the investing public,' he declared. 'I have safeguarded the funds on loan to this company, but I could not commit the crime of offering money for Last Card. My resignation from the board has just been recorded in the minute book.'

He stamped out, slamming the door. Diddle and Shaft rushed after him. Pierpont and Bottle sat staring at the door liked stunned mullets. Spender, his wits sharpened by a lifetime of field audits, dived at Hotfoot to grab back the endorsed cheque and eat it. But Hotfoot – a veteran of financing facility conferences – stopped him with a forearm jolt. 'It wouldn't have been any use, anyway,' he added soothingly. 'They've still got my deposit slip.'

Diddle and Shaft returned disconsolately. 'He won't listen to reason,' wailed Diddle. 'He keeps saying God told him to resign,' said Shaft.

'He seemed to object to blatant fraud,' said Bottle. 'Did you try suggesting we could change this into an unblatant fraud by interposing a few intermediaries?'

Diddle, who had been reading Swizzle's final entry in the minute book, said: 'We've got a bigger problem than you think. Under Rockbound's articles of association, the quorum for a directors' meeting is three. Swizzle has recorded his resignation and also the fact that the board meeting has been left without a quorum. We can't buy the mine. In fact, we can't transact any further business at all.'

'Call in one of your other directors,' cried Spender, whose face had turned a delicate shade of green.

'There aren't any others,' said Shaft.

'Well appoint a new director. And quickly.'

'We can't. We haven't got a quorum.'

'Then for Christ's sake, give us our cheque back.'

'We can't. We haven't got a quorum. We can't do anything.'

They picked up their minute book and walked out, followed discreetly by Hotfoot. The rest of us sat stunned, except for Bottle. Using his engineering experience, Bottle picked the lock on the drinks bar and pulled out a bottle of Teachers.

Since then we have drunk enough Teachers to float an oil tanker, but without finding a solution to the dilemma. Rockbound is in Catch 22. Without a quorum, its board cannot do anything and cannot even get itself a quorum so it can do anything. It is in permanent suspended animation, perhaps for the rest of eternity.

Blue Sky is going to have to announce a $1 million loss instead of break-even. Worse, it owes $5 million to The Hungry Bank and has no hope of retrieving its $5 million loan from Rockbound in the foreseeable future. Even Blue Sky's notoriously pliant audit firm of Halt & Lame will have no choice but to insist on a bad debt provision, which will bring Blue Sky's loss to $6 million, which is sufficient to put the company in chancery.

And that's why you haven't seen the Blue Sky accounts yet. We are just sitting here very quietly, with our heads down, breathing softly and hoping everybody forgets we exist.

BASER AND BASER

Any day now, Blue Sky Mines is going to announce a major base metal discovery. Pierpont can tell readers this with a clear conscience because he has already cornered the available stock.

As a director of Blue Sky, Pierpont has been following a set strategy for the past two decades.

When the market is low, Pierpont first soaks up the stock and then decides what minerals to find. Some punters prefer to wait until a company has found minerals and then buy the stock, but this is an unscientific approach.

The Official History of Blue Sky Mines

In the present case, having got set through various Liberian and Grand Cayman front companies, Pierpont next needed to obtain the help of Bottle the geologist, who would actually make the discovery. This proved no small problem because Bottle has hardly been sober this financial year.

Foolishly, the board allowed him to go to a geologists' seminar in Kalgoorlie where he became so instilled with the camaraderie of the fraternity that he was speechless for a fortnight.

Then, before we could drag him back to civilisation, he went on a field trip to the Northern Territory which was so intensive — especially around Tennant Creek — that he had to spend the next six weeks in a drying out clinic.

Pierpont was waiting at the clinic gate in his Rolls-Royce when Bottle was discharged, and rushed him straight to the Croesus Club for a restorative lunch. We sat Bottle at a table and the steward thoughtfully placed a jug of mineral water in front of him, but his eye went straight past it to Pierpont's bottle of Grand Anné and the next thing your correspondent knew he was ordering seconds.

Between gulps, Bottle could hear Pierpont well enough to grasp the situation which, after all, has happened before in Blue Sky's history.

'We thought of making a good gold discovery,' Pierpont concluded. 'But coming on top of Karpa Spring that might attract unwelcome attention.'

By now the gleam of intelligence had returned to Bottle's eye, nourished by a couple of bottles of brain food from the village of Ay.

'No,' he declared. 'We've found gold too often.'

'Well, we can hardly do rare earths again,' said Pierpont. 'Remember the CAC inquiry of '86?'

'Let's stick to the mainstream of Australian geological practice this time,' suggested Bottle. 'We'll use inferred reserves.'

'Good idea,' mused Pierpont. 'The punters never seem to realise that the word "inferred" stands for "guessed".'

'Not quite,' corrected Bottle. 'But if, for example, you strike mineralisation on ground which is an extension of a known orebody you are entitled to infer that you may have struck a recurrence of that orebody.'

'Until some damned fool drills it,' said Pierpont.

Bottle quickly sketched his plan on the serviette. Broken Hill has a base metal orebody that runs roughly north-south. So does Mount Isa. They are – very roughly – in line. (If you look at a map in Bottle's usual condition they *are* in line).

He will peg some ground wherever it is cheapest on a straight line between them – just east of Birdsville looks the most probable because there is a pub within half an hour's drive – drill a few percussion holes and salt them. (Blue Sky has never drilled an unsalted hole in its history. We do not believe in wasting shareholders' funds on random results when we can ensure definite ones.)

Having encountered some good grades, Bottle will postulate a theory (which, being quite original, should earn him a PhD) that Birdsville East is an extension of Broken Hill or Mount Isa or both and infer that the reserves could match those of Hilton. And it will

The Official History of Blue Sky Mines

all be quite legal, because nobody yet in Australia has been sent to jail for drawing an inference.

And Bottle will make sure that the reserves are inferred at a deep enough level for us to bank the cheques before the next drillhole tests the theory.

After the Great Crash

TECHNICAL BRIEF 4

HOW TO CONDUCT BOARD MEETINGS

By now readers must have realised that the board meetings of Blue Sky Mines are one of the great joys of Pierpont's life.

Our chairman Sir Mark sits at the head of the table, contentedly puffing on a Davidoff, with his mind a perfect blank.

Spender the accountant and Penwiper the secretary compare golf handicaps, while at the far end Bottle the geologist and Pierpont usually manage to corner the Glendronach decanter on its third circuit.

We take a quick scan of the monthly accounts to make sure we are not stealing too much from the company, approve a statement telling a few cursory lies to the ASX, then adjourn for a long, relaxing lunch at the Croesus Club.

The best part is on the way out, when we collect from Penwiper the envelopes containing our attendance fees.

It must be confessed that modern enlightened thought frowns on this sort of meeting. If you listen to all the frightfully earnest chaps at management colleges, law firms and the NCSC, we should only tell the ASX the truth (which would come as a terrible shock to our shareholders) and Penwiper should stop forging the directors' signatures (which means the poor chap would have to wait for them all to turn up sober one day).

Still, some purpose is served by the way Blue Sky's directors meet. Except for Sir Mark, who is deliberately kept in a state of total ignorance, the rest of the board are completely au fait with the company's affairs. And we all turn up at meetings because each of us knows that if one is absent, the others would rob him blind. Nor do we ever blindly approve of plans put forward by the management, because there aren't any plans. Nor is there any management.

The Australian Shareholders' Association probably disapproves of Blue Sky because directors collect fat fees without ever deciding anything at meetings except to make predatory raids on shareholders and the market.

Nevertheless, Pierpont will defend our policy of idleness by pointing out that Australia needs fewer board decisions rather than more. If the directors of Bond Corporation, for example, had done nothing throughout the 1980s, the company would have avoided about $5 billion in losses.

Unfortunately Blue Sky has never got around to producing a manual laying down board procedure or your correspondent might have sent a copy to the old Beneficial Finance Corporation, because the chaps over in Adelaide seemed to have needed a little guidance in the 1980s. Reading the last half a dozen volumes of Auditor-General Ken McPherson's report into BFC's affairs, Pierpont could not help noticing that the financier used to conduct a great number of urgent meetings.

One meeting was held in such a rush that only three directors were able to attend. The opinion of the rest were sought by telephone beforehand, except for Tim Marcus Clark, who was overseas.

Pierpont has always thought that talking to one director at a time is an unsatisfactory way to decide anything. An objection may be made by one director which the others had not thought of, and would support. 'Round-robin' phone calls to directors will therefore always tend to result in approval for whatever is being proposed in head office.

At the meeting to which Pierpont refers, Beneficial decided to proceed with a joint venture to develop the old fruit and vegetable markets in Adelaide. This was one of the worst decisions ever taken by Beneficial and ultimately cost the financier more than $30 million. Rather than holding an urgent board meeting to grab this hot opportunity, the directors would have been better off playing billiards.

Some meetings weren't held at all. McPherson reported that Beneficial had developed a practice some time before 1982 of holding 'paper meetings' of directors.

Minutes were drawn up by the company secretary and signed by the chairman to document decisions which were required to be made by the directors but which in fact were not.

The board normally met on the first Friday of the month, but McPherson found there was frequently a need for directors to approve transactions at other times. The practice adopted by Beneficial was not to convene a meeting to give the necessary approvals but simply to produce minutes as though such a meeting had been held. The minutes were sometimes included in the papers for the next regular board meeting, but they were usually not discussed and rarely was the decision of the paper meeting referred to in the minutes of a subsequent regular meeting.

McPherson counted a total of 23 paper meetings between January 1988 and July 1989. One of them approved the purchase of $116 million in receivables from the Equiticorp group, which could only be categorised as a high-risk deal. It was not until April 1989 that the board demanded proper notification of all meetings, including the paper ones.

Considering that nearly half of Beneficial's portfolio eventually required some form of provisioning, Pierpont is prepared to wager that many of the decisions taken at urgent and paper meetings resulted in losses.

Indeed, management at Beneficial also developed a habit of approving and settling deals, then getting board approval later. The justification was that some other lender might steal the precious deal from Beneficial if they waited until the regular monthly board meeting.

In one such deal, Beneficial management established a joint venture with Mortgage Acceptance Corporation which had actually begun operations before the board was asked to approve the deal. This deal resulted in Beneficial developing an exposure of more than $100 million to a joint venture which was operated by the other partner. By May 1991 an internal audit found that 63 per cent of the joint venture portfolio was in arrears and a provision of $10 million had to be raised to cover losses.

Given the state of the law these days, directors face pretty stiff penalties for the misdemeanours of their companies.

At Blue Sky Mines, the directors have decided that any misdemeanours will be committed personally by the directors. If we ever go to jail (a pretty long shot, given the inefficiencies of the DPP), it will at least be for our own actions and not those of management.

Paper meetings are a particularly dubious idea. You don't even get near the Glendronach decanter.

Pierpont's MINING GAME

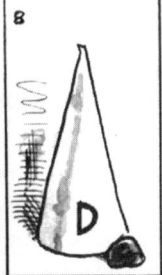

THE MARKET IS RISING, MINING IS FASHIONABLE...

GO

1 EUPHORIA! HAVE A BOTTLE OF BOLLINGER

2 BUY A MINER'S RIGHT. SEND $10 TO THE STATE GOVERNMENT

7 FLOAT SUCCESSFUL. COLLECT $1M AND RETURN TO GO (THIS IS THE ONLY PROFITABLE SEQUENCE IN THE GAME)

8 EXPLORE PROSPECT SPEND $½M

9 ASSAY LAB LOSES DRILL CORES. SPEND ANOTHER $½M EXPLORING

10 EUREKA! ASSAYS SHOW VIABLE GRADES. THROW A PARTY AND MOLEST SECRETARY

15-20 SACRED SITE. SPEND NINE YEARS HAGGLING (ALL PLAYERS PROCEEDING PAST SQUARE 7 MUST LAND ON THIS SQUARE AT SOME POINT. IT IS IMPOSSIBLE TO HAVE A MINE WITHOUT A SACRED SITE)

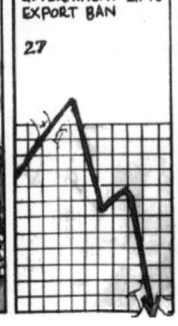

25 BORROW $3M. BANK MANAGER FROWNS

26 STRIKE WATERTABLE SINKING SHAFT SPEND $5M

27 METAL PRICES FALL GOVERNMENT LIFTS EXPORT BAN

28 MINE OPENS, MAKING MARGINAL LOSS

PEG CLAIM 3	**OVER-PEGGING DISPUTE. MISS ONE TURN WHILE BRIBING OTHER LITIGANT** 4	**ISSUE PROSPECTUS. MISS TWO TURNS ANSWERING CAC INQUIRIES** 5	**FLOAT COMPANY... PAY $100,000 TO BROKER** 6
HANGOVER. LAB REPORTS ERROR IN ASSAYS 11	**SPEND ANOTHER $½M ON EXPLORATION** 12	**SECRETARY PREGNANT. WIFE FILES FOR DIVORCE. SETTLE WITH SCRIP** 13	**GRADES AND TONNAGES CONFIRMED VIABLE. YOU HAVE A MINE.** 14
NEGOTIATE CONTRACT WITH JAPANESE. BANK MANAGER SMILES! 21	**METAL PRICES BOOM. GOVERNMENT BANS EXPORTS. SPEND SIX MONTHS IN CANBERRA** 22	**CONSERVATIONISTS PROTEST. PROCEED TO NEXT SQUARE** 23	**CHANGE MINE FROM OPEN-CUT TO UNDERGROUND TO PRESERVE HABITAT OF HAIRY-NOSED BANDICOOT. COSTS MULTIPLY BY 4.** 24
JAPANESE TEAR UP CONTRACT (THEY CLAIM MINE IS 5 YEARS LATE OPENING) 29	**STRIKE. WINCHDRIVERS WALK OUT, DEMANDING 1½ HOUR WEEK** 30		

5

THE 1990s AND THE RECESSION WE JUST HAD TO HAVE

~

*T*he 1990s started with Paul Keating's very own recession. Blue Sky, as usual, kept on swindling shareholders regardless of the state of the economy.

The empires of the corporate cowboys collapsed as their creditors moved in. One of the first to move was Kerry Packer, wrenching Channel 9 back from Alan Bond.

The gold price drifted under $US330 by the start of 1993, jumped back to $US400 and then drifted sideways uncertainly.

The all ordinaries managed to get back to 2300 in 1993 and then went sideways too.

In 1990 the NCSC was replaced by the Australian Securities Commission, which was even more vigilant at suppressing corporate crime.

MacArthur River was on the verge of development, but somehow had not actually quite been mined yet.

One-Way Preference Shares

Every investor in Australia must by now be aware of the brawl between Bond Media and Consolidated Press Holdings over the proposed treatment of Bond's preference shares. Indeed, in view of the publicity it has been given in the Australian press so far in 1990, Pierpont has no doubt that kangaroos in the Petermann Ranges are by now fully conversant with Bond Media's debt structure and discuss the finer points around waterholes at sunset.

But for the benefit of anyone who has spent the past year on Mars, Bond Media has $200 million in convertible redeemable preference shares held by Consolidated Press Holdings. They are now due to be either converted or redeemed. As the conversion price is $4.65 per share and Bond Media last sold at 12c, even a mentally retarded kangaroo would not opt for conversion.

CPH wants to redeem the shares and collect its $200 million. (Alternatively, CPH has offered to take over Bond Media through a vehicle called Television Corp of Australia, but that is irrelevant to Pierpont's argument today.)

Bond Media is saying: 'No. You cannot pass Go. You cannot collect 200. Go back to Park Lane.' (Or, in Conspress's case, Park Street.) Bond Media is claiming in the WA courts that it is legally forbidden from redeeming the shares because of the provisions of Section 120(3) of the Companies Code.

Section 120(3)(b) provides that redeemable preference shares shall not be redeemed except out of profits that would otherwise be available for dividends or out of the proceeds of a fresh share issue made to fund the redemption. Section 120(4) further provides that any premium payable on redemption shall be provided for out of profits or out of the share premium reserve. By implication, therefore, Pierpont would guess that Section 120(3)(b) applies only to the capital element of the preference shares.

The preference shares held by CPH comprise 200,000 $1 shares issued at a premium of $999 each. In other words their capital element ts $200,000 and the premium is $199,800,000. Bond Media, as Pierpont understands its argument, is claiming it cannot redeem the shares until it makes an equivalent profit.

The Official History of Blue Sky Mines

In the year to June 1989, Bond Media declared an after tax loss of $2.8 million plus extraordinary losses of $50.6 million. In the latest six months to December it reported a net profit after tax of $274,000 but this blew to a loss of $32 million after taking in extraordinary write-offs.

As fascinated spectators of this game, Pierpont's colleagues at Blue Sky Mines are frankly cheering for Bondy.

The reason is not hard to see. If a learned judge upholds the Bond case, Blue Sky will immediately issue all the redeemable preference shares it can ($200 million would do fine). If the law says that they can only be redeemed out of profits, readers can rest assured that Blue Sky will never, ever declare another profit. We might even call them one-way preference shares.

Having said all that Pierpont hastens to add that the latest evidence shows Alan Bond to be a man of honour, or at least of greater commercial honour than the average receiver. Your correspondent discovered this over a few special cuvee bruts at the Bollinger Trophy dinner the other night. The trophy, for the top racehorse owner, went to Robert Sangster's Swettenham Stud for the third consecutive year.

Pierpont applauded politely, but felt deep down that the trophy should perhaps have gone to William Inglis & Son for becoming the potential owner of some of Bart Cummings' horse debts after last year's sales.

This is by the way, however. What really riveted Pierpont was the news that Alan Bond had ordered a crate of Bollinger last December after winning the Sydney-Hobart. This seemed to Pierpont and others a terrible risk by the vendors at the time, but Alan paid the bill on December 28 – the day before the National Australia Bank put the receivers in. A gentleman pays his wine bills, you see.

Encouraged by this, the Bollinger people kept supplying bubbly to Bond Brewing while it was in receivership but now the receivers have departed without paying their bill.

Shame, shame.

LAST RITES FOR LAST CARD

It was a funereal meeting last week of the board of Blue Sky Mines (No Liability Except At Gunpoint). We put a wreath above the gin

The 1990s and the Recession We Just Had to Have

cupboard and tied little black crepe ribbons around our Cohiba coronas. It is always sad to lose an old friend, but the time had come. We were conducting the last rites for the Last Card tungsten mine.

Pierpont could scant repress a tear as Penwiper – our poor but dishonest secretary – read the motion to write off Last Card to zero and declare it abandoned. Of course, your correspondent knows it's just a barren waste of granite and bulldust with a few scurvy scratchings on the surface whenever we wanted to convince Perth analysts spying from helicopters that work was in progress but, to Pierpont, Last Card was an old, true friend.

Over the two decades that Last Card has been Blue Sky's prime – indeed, sole – asset, we have announced viable tungsten grades 13 times, viable molybdenum grades four times, viable rare earth grades three times and viable gold grades once (the night Bottle the geologist was too drunk to spell 'molybdenum').

According to Blue Sky's announcements to the stock exchanges we have also sunk 27 drill holes on Last Card, dug 114 costeans and started sinking 11 shafts. If any nosy parker were to visit the remote location and see no sign of any such activity, Bottle would have explained that we are dedicated to environmental restoration. Last

Card has also, when it suited us to dampen the market, had three careers as a sacred site.

Last Card of course contains no more tungsten than you would find in a gum tree and was indeed carefully selected because it was entirely innocent of mineralisation, thus allowing us to give free rein to our imaginations.

We have run the shares from half a cent to $2 and back again, playing the stock like a zither. It has made us enough money to fund Occidental Insurance's deficiency (were we foolish enough to do so) and in the process has given several lucky employees of the Corporate Affairs Commission pretty suntans as they searched our register for nominee companies from Grand Cayman, the Cook Islands, Panama, Liberia and other tropical resorts.

But, alas! The good times don't last forever, and the new Australian Securities Commission was getting dangerously close to our scent. Our accounting policy has long been that the value of Last Card rises every year. To stop this figure reaching infinity, however, we achieve this by reducing the previous year's figure. Thus in 1989, its value rose from $1 million to $1.5 million, while in 1990 its value rose from $1.2 million to $1.6 million.

For 20 years, nobody has ever read the previous year's accounts to compare the figures. But last week an ASC sleuth rang to ask how the same mine on the same day was worth either $1.5 million or $1.2 million depending on whether you read the 1989 or the 1990 accounts. Penwiper pleaded alcoholism, which in the case of the Blue Sky board is a good fighting defence, but it was clear that only drastic action would remove the threat.

So we're writing it off. It was an emotional moment which even moved our chairman, that old dunderhead Sir Mark Time.

'You have my sympathy,' he said to Bottle. 'I had to admire the way you soldiered on year after year with Last Card, despite all those confusing assay reports. It's been a devilishly tricky orebody, but you showed grit in persevering with it.'

'Hear, hear,' chimed in Spender the accountant. 'I'd say Bottle is the sort of prospector who's made Australian mining what it is today.' A tear rose to Bottle's eye – or it might have been some of the gin leaking out – and he croaked a husky thank you.

'But we should not be too melancholy,' he told Sir Mark. 'Because we've made an exciting new discovery in the same region.'

To say this was paltering with the truth would be like describing Saddam Hussein as a Tel Aviv demolition contractor. About the most exciting discovery you could make within a hundred miles of Last Card would be a dead bandicoot.

What happened, readers will be relieved to know, is that we simply couldn't bear to let Last Card go. So we've repegged it under a different name. We'll move the dot on the map in the annual report a fraction to the right and have a whole new mine.

'That's great news!' exclaimed Sir Mark. 'What's it called?'

'It's an old working called the Endless Shaft,' said Bottle. 'There doesn't seem to be any trace of it in the Mines Department records, but I have sworn statements from old prospectors about the ore they extracted from it.' (The most expensive part of the exploration program was finding two prospectors who were prepared to sign the statement, because part of the deal was that they had to leave home immediately and depart for the Gold Coast with no forwarding addresses. Anyhow, we have a new mine and Last Card – sorry, Endless Shaft – can start its 20-year life cycle over again.)

'Splendid news!' cried Sir Mark. 'I must be off to tell the chaps at the club.' He was at the door before a thought struck him. 'By the way,' he asked. 'What kind of mine is it?'

This was a subject that had taken long discussion at an earlier caucus between Bottle, Spender, Penwiper and Pierpont. Penwiper wanted to make it a molybdenum mine because that might have some dim credibility. Pierpont promptly scotched the idea on the twin grounds that (a) as there were absolutely no valuable minerals at Endless Shaft we might as well make it something exciting, and (b) molybdenum had been out of fashion since 1974 with no return in sight. And nobody knows what it is, anyway.

'It must be something fashionable,' said Pierpont. (In his youth, your correspondent was told by a Toronto stockbroker: 'If the mob want apples, sell them apples. If you haven't got apples, get oranges and paint them green'. It is one of the maxims Pierpont has lived by ever since.)

Spender wanted to make it an oil field. This was attractive because (a) oil is highly volatile in price, (b) oil exploration lends itself to misleading statements quite as well as metal mining, and (c) oil is currently fashionable and likely to stay fashionable as long as there is trouble in the Gulf. As the Gulf has so far been troublesome for 6000 years, prospects are excellent.

However, there are almost no onshore wildcat wells in Australia. Endless Shaft would stick out like a sore thumb every time it made an announcement. So we abandoned Endless Shaft as an oilfield.

In the present markets, nothing else quite filled the bill. The base metals are interesting without being exciting and gold looks as though it is going to sleep again. Coal is prospering but a coal deposit won't move a stock two cents.

Being democrats, the four of us finally settled the question by a vote. The result of the poll was:

Copper 2
Gold 1
Uranium . . . 1

'Well,' said Bottle, replying to Sir Mark. 'It looks as though it could be a second Roxby Downs.'

'Marvellous,' burbled Sir Mark. 'We're doing our bit for Australia.'

THE GREAT SACRED GIN CUPBOARD

The directors of Blue Sky Mines were an unprepossessing sight as the board meeting opened.

The day before had seen the Grand Annual Tour of the Croesus Club cellars and the impact was still visible.

Sir Mark Time was sitting ashen at the head of the table, his eyes gazing sightlessly into the middle distance and looking as though a trainee undertaker had just embalmed him in gelatine.

Spender the accountant was emitting low moaning noises and leaning at 45 degrees to the desk blotter. Pierpont, whose cranium had been occupied overnight by a gang of riveters, was trying to focus on the agenda.

All of us looked like Olympic athletes compared to Bottle the geologist. Bottle had spent two nights in the Ironclad Hotel at Marble Bar negotiating claims with prospectors, then flown back to the east coast via Port Hedland, Dampier, Perth and the Red Eye Special, a

The 1990s and the Recession We Just Had to Have

trip which even a Salvation Army chaplain could not undertake without massive alcoholic stimulants.

The standard procedure when a board is incompetent, derelict, hung over or otherwise incapacitated would be for the company secretary to take over the meeting. Indeed, Pierpont imagines the majority of board meetings in Australia are conducted this way.

But in Blue Sky's case it was not an option. Penwiper, our poor but dishonest secretary, believed that the share market was suffering a technical correction when the all ordinaries bounced up to 1250 in January. So he started selling Share Price Index contracts and has been continuing to sell them all the way to 1550.

He is now up to the fourth mortgage on the family home, unbeknown to Mrs Penwiper, and is easing the pain by drinking a few bottles of neat tequila every night. The rest of the board are running a calcutta on which will happen first out of (a) cirrhosis, (b) bankruptcy, or (c) a homicide by Mrs Penwiper when she discovers all.

When the board met, Penwiper was looking in worse shape than usual. He had forgotten to buy a lemon on the way home and was still suffering from tequila aftertaste.

So the directors were forced to grapple with Blue Sky's latest crisis themselves. The crisis is that a few foolhardy punters suddenly got enthusiastic about Blue Sky's Endless Shaft gold prospect and have been buying Blue Sky shares, pushing the price from 5c to 15c.

This threatens a catastrophe for Spender, Pierpont and Bottle, who have been heavily short Blue Sky through an unscrupulous London broker. The question now was how we could defuse the market and get Blue Sky shares down so we could cover our short positions.

Spender's moans gradually took coherent shape. 'What we need is a sacred site,' he croaked. 'If Bula the Spirit can stop Coronation Hill, which has actually got some real gold, it shouldn't take much of a spirit to stop Endless Shaft.'

Pierpont glanced nervously at Sir Mark, to whom truth is best dispensed in very small doses, if at all. But Sir Mark had sunk into a cataleptic trance. Either the '48 Grange or the '52 St Henri, Pierpont reckoned.

'But where can we get a sacred site?' whispered Pierpont.

'Shacred Shite? Eashy!' slurred Bottle. 'Pick one up in Arnhem Land with a front-end loader. Truck it acrosh in coupla daysh.'

'Or we could pick up Noonkanbah's Rainbow Serpent,' suggested Pierpont. 'It hasn't been used in years.'

'Too expensive,' frowned Spender. 'Just borrow a D-8 and push a few rocks together into a formation. My nephew's studying anthropology so I'll get him to put together a legend about the Bandicoot Dreaming.'

'Will he cost much?' asked Pierpont.

'Maybe a box of crayons,' said Spender. 'He's only four.'

'Good idea,' mused Pierpont. 'When we finish with our sacred site we could sell it to someone else.'

By this time Bottle had cracked open the Great Sacred Gin Cupboard. A legend going back to Dreamtime (1972) says that from this cupboard a spirit emerges that causes distress and devastation.

'Heart shtarter?' he offered.

That snapped Sir Mark back to life. 'Don't mind if I do,' he said. 'Did I miss anything when I dropped off?'

'Not yet,' said Spender, hunting in his drawer for the Rainbow Corkscrew.

GETTING TO THE CORE OF THE PROBLEM

An experienced eye could have seen at a glance that this was a real board meeting of Blue Sky Mines. The directors were tolerably sober, there were no minute books on the table and our figurehead chairman, Sir Mark time, was absent.

Actually Sir Mark was due to stroll through the door in half an hour to start what he thought was the real board meeting. We had given ourselves 30 minutes for a preliminary caucus to sort out the latest problem in our company's chequered career.

On the Pierpont Problem Rating Scale, which ranks a late annual return as one, and appointment of a receiver as 10, the present problem rated around four. That put it ahead of justifying Bottle the geologist's field expenses to the Tax Office (three) but well below losing the key to the gin cupboard (nine).

The 1990s and the Recession We Just Had to Have

Spender the accountant waited until the Chivas Regal decanter had completed the first circuit of the table and called our little meeting to order. 'I thought we had encountered every problem known to man in this company, but today we've struck an unexpected one,' he asserted. 'The assay laboratory has developed a conscience.'

Bottle dropped his glass. Pierpont choked on a Davidoff. Penwiper made a sudden blot among the forged signatures he had been practising on his blotter.

Our concern arose because we had recently acquired the Glittering Glass diamond prospect in the Kimberleys. Through our Panamanian trust company, we had gone long Blue Sky shares and were waiting for a favourable assay to send the price up.

Pure routine, you might say. All we needed was a surface sample that would show some indicator minerals such as chrome diopside, pyrope garnet or ilmenite and we could leave the rest to the market. A small but simple exercise in salting. As usual we had sent the sample to Random Result Assay Laboratories and were waiting for the results.

'So what went wrong?' gasped Pierpont. 'Were we low on indicators?'

'We got the indicators all right,' replied Spender. 'But I'm afraid Bottle sent in a drill core instead of a surface sample and the lab wants to know why, because we haven't announced a drilling program.'

This was awkward, but there was room for hope. Given the far fetched stories Randoms had swallowed in the past (in return, we never scrutinise their invoices too closely) they would probably accept any explanation that was halfway reasonable. At least we hadn't done anything as outrageous as salting with an actual diamond.

'I once read in a business manual that your first option should always be to tell the truth,' suggested Penwiper.

'We stole the core from Argyle,' grunted Bottle.

'I wish you'd stop reading fiction,' Spender sighed to Penwiper. 'What's our second option?'

'We could say we found it lying on the surface,' mused Bottle.

'Or that it fell off a passing truck,' added Penwiper brightly.

Pierpont, being the longest married and therefore the most gifted in extemporaneous untruth, had a better solution. 'Why don't we say we hired a rig but it had only spudded in when we discovered that the area was environmentally sensitive for the hairy-nosed bandicoot?' your correspondent suggested. 'But we sent them the sample anyway?'

'What do we say happened to drilling?' asked Spender.

'Suspended while we shoot the bandicoots.'

The table burst into spontaneous applause, just as Sir Mark Time sauntered through the door. 'Good Heavens!' he exclaimed. 'Have I interrupted a celebration?'

'We were just applauding the assay results from Glittering Glass,' Spender said smoothly. 'There's only one small technicality to clear away.'

Sir Mark beamed and took his chair. Bottle poured Pierpont a congratulatory Chivas. Penwiper lifted the minute books onto the table. The formal board meeting was about to begin.

BIG GOANNA FALLS FROM BLUE SKY

Shareholders, in their dumb way, may have noticed that they didn't hear much about the affairs of Blue Sky Mines last year. That is for the excellent reason that we weren't doing anything. It is high policy that Blue Sky never wastes its shareholders' money digging holes in the ground unless the share market is buoyant.

Last year was pretty flat, with the price of just about every metal heading south. As several thousand crows, bandicoots and wallabies could testify, this meant there was no fieldwork done at our mine – which is our loose way of describing the sparsely mineralised patch of wasteland named Endless Shaft which we pegged two decades ago in the middle of Western Australia.

Nor were there many board meetings. Our chairman, Sir Mark Time, spent 1992 in a coma at the Croesus Club. Our poor but dishonest secretary, Penwiper, had a particularly lean year. We only pay him a pittance, on the understanding that he is to make his living from insider trading, but as Blue Sky shares were in the doldrums all year he had to take part-time work as a repossession agent. Given the continuing collapse of the real estate market, this meant he began driving some interesting automobiles.

Blue Sky's treasury suffered a severe cash outflow. Bottle the geologist spent the year on an exploration program in Hannan's Club and the Palace at Kalgoorlie. Spender toured Asia setting up paper

The 1990s and the Recession We Just Had to Have

companies in Taiwan, Korea and Shenzhen and can now boast the investment world's most fashionable addresses on his letterhead.

Pierpont took his bride on a leisurely tour of the Sandwich Islands and might never have returned from The Lodge at Lana'i if Blue Sky's liquids hadn't dried up.

When directors need more spending money, the time-honoured method of raising it is to float a new company. So Blue Sky is spinning off Great Goanna Gold No Liability. The share market isn't much better now than it was six months ago, but if we don't float now the directors will suffer a severe cutback in their lifestyles.

The board meeting to approve this depredation on the investing public was held at the start of the year. Sir Mark, his wits dulled by a year of inactivity, set a new record by gazing at the agenda in black incomprehension for seven minutes before speaking.

'I don't remember Great Goanna,' he finally grumbled, waking Penwiper, who'd been out late the previous night hot-wiring a Porsche. 'When did we acquire it?'

'It was the star asset I picked up on my field trip to Kalgoorlie last year,' smiled Bottle. Actually, the best asset acquired by Bottle on his trip was a diverse and fascinating collection of skimpies' G-strings.

The Official History of Blue Sky Mines

As an afterthought, he had also acquired Great Goanna at the Palace corner bar some time after midnight during Boulder Cup Week. Even though operating purely on his subconscious mind at the time, Bottle realised that Great Goanna was mere scrubland. But it was a terrific address, being right alongside the Mammoth gold deposit owned by A Very Big Company Which Shall Be Nameless.

Sir Mark's mind – or whatever you want to call the collection of shellgrit between his ears – was still turning over slowly. 'Alongside Mammoth,' he breathed. 'Good address.'

Mammoth is a very good deposit, but is being kept under wraps by the Very Big Company because it is negotiating an agreement with the local Aboriginal tribe and waiting for the gold price to go up, upon which it will announce the mine and an issue simultaneously.

This has been very frustrating to Blue Sky. We hoped that the VBC would have declared Mammoth a mine last year so that our float could have enjoyed a free ride on the back of the publicity.

Instead, the VBC has stayed silent. As Mammoth is only one mine in its big portfolio, the company has not been obliged to announce anything.

Sir Mark had finally turned to page four of the prospectus, which was the enticing bit. 'What marvellous assays they've had from Mammoth,' he burbled. 'Ten to 15 grams in four holes . . . close to the surface . . . open at depth and length . . . Marvellous!'

He paused and looked around. 'I must be getting old you know,' he apologised. 'I don't remember any of these assays being announced for Mammoth before.'

We hastened to reassure Sir Mark that precious brain cells such as his should not be clogged by detail. In truth, no assays have been announced on Mammoth by the VBC so Blue Sky, tired of waiting, has filled the gap. Bottle slipped through the fence with a drill and a couple of trusted hands one night and punched a few shallow holes in the orebody. The grades in our prospectus for Mammoth are perfectly accurate.

The only slight technicality that could be raised by a purist is that they are being announced by Blue Sky instead of by the Very Big Company. But this does not make our prospectus false. Indeed, it is more accurate than it would have been otherwise. And the Very Big

Company has so many layers of middle management that with any luck, they'll never notice what we've done.'

'Well, it all looks fine to me,' said Sir Mark, closing the prospectus. 'By the way, whose Porsche was that in the garage?'

'Mine,' replied Penwiper, minuting the unanimous approval of the float.

'Had a bit of luck, eh?' asked Sir Mark.

'Yes,' said Penwiper. 'We've been doing advertising agencies this week.'

A NICE PLACE FOR A PLACEMENT

The decanter of Glendronach having completed its second circuit of the directors' table, the board meeting of Blue Sky Mines was declared open. Our chairman, Sir Mark Time, looked at the agenda and broke into a senile grin.

'I say! You chaps have done well,' he chortled. 'You've raised three quarters of a million. That's enough cash to get us through next year. How did you do it?'

'A share placement,' explained Penwiper. 'A lot of small companies have been making placements lately, sir.'

They have indeed. Hardly a day goes past without a company announcing that it has just placed a few shares. So we reckoned that an announcement of a small, quick placement from Blue Sky could be slipped through without attracting the attention of the regulatory authorities.

'Five million at 15c,' Sir Mark read, labouring over the agenda paper as though it had been written in Sanskrit. 'By Jove! That's as high as the shares went in that run last week.'

It was as high as the shares have been in three years. It was no accident either. Pierpont and Spender have been assiduously dropping hints around the Croesus Club about a big strike at the Endless Shaft mine, while Bottle has been whispering the same rumour around the Palace bar at Kalgoorlic.

Blue Sky had run out of money and we needed to push the price up specifically so we could place a few. A rights issue was out of the question because the board holds currently 70 per cent of the stock. Our policy is to take money out of Blue Sky, not put it in.

'I noticed there was quite a bit of turnover in Blue Sky,' Sir Mark continued. 'Between that and the placement we'll have a few new names on the share register, eh?'

Not as many as he thinks. Actually, the market turnover and the placement were the same thing. A real placement could have been done only by ringing professional investors, which would have taken a lot of time and trouble – and then they would have been too smart to take up the shares for more than a few cents. So we had reverted to an old nickel boom practice and placed the shares on-market. The buyers who had raced out into the market did not know it, but they were buying previously unissued scrip from our vaults.

The only technical drawback to this method of placing shares is that it is illegal. The Rae Report on the nickel boom was highly critical of on-market placements by VAM, North Deborah, Swan Brewery and others. The regulators hold the view that the punters are entitled to know how many shares a company has on issue when they are investing. But Pierpont and Spender are quite sure that the would-be insiders who rushed out and bought the stock were just trying to make a quick killing and neither knew nor cared how many shares there were supposed to be in Blue Sky.

Sir Mark frowned, an indication that two of his brain cells were now working. 'One thing about this,' he said. 'Our percentage holding in Blue Sky will be diluted by the placement, so I hope none of you chaps were selling or we'll be diluted even further.'

'Our holdings are undisturbed, Sir Mark,' Spender murmured soothingly. 'You shouldn't worry about a thing.'

There is even less to worry about than he thinks. Issued capital having risen to 60 million shares, our next move in a few months' time will be to announce a consolidation. Every five shares now issued will be merged into one share. By that time the share price will have fallen again. The recent buyers, aghast at the thought of their stock being reduced to unmarketable small parcels, will dump the stock and push the price down even further.

If the stock does not fall quickly enough, we will issue a statement about the Endless Shaft mine, telling something close to the truth about its prospects. As the shares slide the main buyer will be Leo Liability the stockbroker, acting on behalf of Spender, Bottle and Pierpont.

At the end of the day our equity in Blue Sky should be exactly where it was before. It will involve a small outlay but we can, after all, afford it. We have just had a windfall of $750,000.

FOLLOWING THE GOVERNMENT'S LEAD

Sir Mark Time had been staring at the board meeting agenda for so long that the rest of the directors thought he had slipped into terminal coma. Finally, he found speech.

'I'm not sure I understand this share issue we're proposing' he apologised. 'I must be getting dense.'

'Oh no, Sir Mark, you're not getting dense,' Spender the accountant reassured him, putting a trifle too much emphasis on the word 'getting'. Spender gave our figurehead chairman his accountant's smile, economically razor-thin with just the tips of his sharp teeth showing. 'This is not an issue of new shares by Blue Sky. It's a sale of existing shares by tender.'

Pierpont and Bottle the accountant, down the end of the board table near the Macallan decanter, could hear the cogs grinding as this idea worked its way through what, for want of a better word, might be called Sir Mark's mind. Time stood still, as it often does at meetings of Blue Sky's geriatric board. Bottle poured himself a fresh four fingers while Pierpont extracted a Davidoff from his cigar case and carefully began removing the band. After about five minutes, Sir Mark spoke again.

'Well, if Blue Sky's not selling the shares, who is?' he asked plaintively.

'Bottle, Pierpont and myself have accumulated about 40 per cent of Blue Sky through the exercise of options,' explained Spender. 'We're selling half of it by tender. We are asking institutions to bid for 10 per cent and we're prepared to sell the other 10 per cent to the public for five cents under the institutional bid price.'

Time stood still even longer as Sir Mark grappled with the concept. Pierpont was contemplating his most important decision of the day. Should he clip the Davidoff or pierce it? Bottle lowered his malt and poured an even larger one. The only sounds were Sir Mark's

The Official History of Blue Sky Mines

grinding cog wheels and the scratching of a nib as Penwiper practised forging the directors' signatures.

The institutional bid will of course be led by a Swiss bank, operating for a Hong Kong trust controlled by a Jersey company whose beneficial owners are Bottle, Spender and Pierpont.

Blue Sky shares were 40c when we exercised our options but a little mysterious buying has pushed them to 80c on rumours of the tender. The institution will bid $1.20 but no actual money will change hands because we will simply be buying 10 per cent of the company from ourselves.

The real sting is in the blind tender to the public. All the punters who line up to get their stock five cents below the institutional price will find they have paid $1.15 a share for a company which – if ever truthfully audited – would disclose a deficiency in shareholders' funds.

'But when you sell shares, don't you have to nominate a price?' asked Sir Mark. 'These chaps will be just sending us cheques without knowing what price we're going to sell the shares to them.'

'It's perfectly legal,' said Spender. 'It's exactly the same as the current sale of Commonwealth Bank shares by the federal government. We've copied their prospectus almost word for word.'

Sir Mark picked up the Blue Sky prospectus, looking – as he often does when handling Blue Sky documents – as though he wished he had a pair of tongs. 'It seems a very skinny prospectus,' he gruffed. He flicked through it desultorily.

If Sir Mark was going to try to read, we had time to refill the decanter. Pierpont took the big decision and pierced his corona, then lit it with a long wooden match, leaned back and inhaled a lungful of expensively refreshing smoke. 'Aren't we supposed to put a lot of figures in a prospectus,' fretted Sir Mark. 'Showing our latest accounts and giving forecasts and all that?'

'The Commonwealth didn't,' responded Spender. 'They just said anyone who wanted to look at figures could go find a copy of their annual report. We've said the same.'

'And there's nothing for you to worry about,' intervened Pierpont. 'The prospectus is issued by the three of us, not by Blue Sky. This meeting is purely informational.'

Sir Mark's face lit up. 'You mean I don't have to do anything?' he beamed.

Bottle, with a quart of Macallan inside him by now, beamed back. 'We never want to put you to trouble, Sir Mark,' he said.

'Fine,' burbled Sir Mark. 'But I hope you chaps aren't taking a risk.'

'Don't worry,' said Spender. 'There's a paragraph saying that we do not guarantee the investment. We copied that one from the government, too.'

DON'T WORRY, THIS WON'T HURT A BIT

The dunderheaded chairman of Blue Sky Mines No Liability, Sir Mark Time, was frowning – nay, scowling – as he read the draft chairman's address for the annual meeting. Finally, after a few coughs and splutters, he found speech.

'I say, chaps!' he exclaimed, breathing stentoriously, 'I know we've been a bit rough on the shareholders in the past, but this time we seem to be taking it too far.'

Spender, being an accountant, was as usual ready with a smooth rationalisation. 'I wouldn't worry much about shareholders, Sir

Mark,' he murmured. 'I would have thought we'd proved years ago that their capacity to stand pain is almost infinite.'

'True,' conceded Sir Mark. 'But I can't help feeling that a few of them may be human. Do you really think they'll stand for these super shares?'

Those readers who are fortunate enough not to hold Blue Sky stock may need a little background at this point. The board of Blue Sky – ever eager to follow a trend set by leaders of Australian commerce – has decided to issue shares with super voting rights.

'We're just falling in with the fashion and issuing shares carrying 25 times the voting rights of the existing ordinary shares,' explained Spender. 'And all shareholders can subscribe on a one-for-20 basis, so it's quite equitable.'

'But the premium seems high at $1', complained Sir Mark. 'While the shares are only 50 cents.'

'Fifty-five actually,' said Spender. 'And we believe in the argument that shares with super voting rights should carry a premium.'

This was stretching the truth to rubbery limits even by the standards of the accounting profession. Bottle the geologist has recently been spreading a rumour around the marketplace that our main prospect – the Endless Shaft mine – has become economic. In this credulous market, punters will believe anything and so have been buying the stock. They've been buying a lot of it from Bottle, Pierpont and Spender, who have unloaded almost their entire 40 per cent holding in Blue Sky onto wood ducks in the past fortnight.

The announcement of a $1 issue will stop the market in its tracks. Then our September quarter report from Endless Shaft will be a disaster (all we have to do is tell the truth for once). The shareholders will no longer he interested in the voting rights of their shares, but only in how quickly they can sell them.

It won't matter much, because the super issue has been underwritten by a Hong Kong trust which fronts for a Panamanian company controlled by a blind Jersey nominee company whose secret beneficial holders are Pierpont, Bottle and Spender.

Having unloaded our 40 per cent at an average of better than 50c, we can easily afford to pick up five per cent of the company (it's a one-for-20, remember) at $1. Even if a few certifiable lunatics subscribe to the shares, we will still hold effective control of the company with only four per cent of the capital, because the super shares have voting rights of 25 for one.

Sir Mark still had the dumbly mutinous air of a racehorse that won't take its etorphine.

'Are there any benefits to the shareholders?' he asked.

'Not only do they get an equal right to participate,' Spender smiled winningly, 'but the existing ordinary shares will have priority to dividends over the super shares.'

Of course, as long as Pierpont and his band of geriatric larcenists are in charge of Blue Sky, it has no chance of paying a dividend this side of the next Ice Age, but Sir Mark overlooked this technicality. His brow was still furrowed.

'How do our institutional holders feel?' he asked, pen poised over the document.

'Our institutional shareholders . . .' said Spender (Pierpont wondered whom he was talking about, but quickly worked out that he must have meant shareholders who were inside institutions.) 'Our institutional shareholders have indicated support. A major Hong Kong institution is underwriting the issue.'

'Jolly good,' beamed Sir Mark.

'And you must remember,' pressed Spender, 'that to the extent super shares are held by management, it will enable Blue Sky to continue under the guidance and leadership that have made the company what it is today.'

'Well, the shareholders can't possibly object to that,' exclaimed Sir Mark and signed with a flourish.'

AN ANOMALY NOT QUITE ALONG THE RIGHT LINES

When the board meeting of Blue Sky Mines opened, our chairman, that old fathead Sir Mark Time, was beaming happily – a certain sign he didn't understand what was happening. 'I understand you chaps have made a big discovery at Starving Wombat,' he burbled. 'I can't wait to hear about it.'

Everyone else was prepared to wait a long time. Indeed, there was a silence lasting half a chukka as the rest of us pondered who should tell the first lie of the meeting. Spender, being an accountant and hardened to mendacity, volunteered.

'Yes, Sir Mark,' he said. 'Our diligent exploration program has paid off.'

On a scale of untruths where 'Your cheque is in the mail' rates as one, and 'I never saw that woman before in my life' rates 10, Spender's statement crossed the bar at about 7.5. Starving Wombat is a barren patch of wasteland in the middle of Western Australia which we refer to as a scheelite prospect whenever we need a good laugh.

We had been pretending to take surface tests along the boundary of the mining company next door, trying to spy on their drill rig, and our field hand had taken a few resistivity tests (which measure differences in electric charges in rocks below) just to add colour to the espionage attempt.

Later, reading the results, the chap noticed we had detected an area of high resistivity. This got everyone interested. Resistivity indicates a geological anomaly which might contain viable mineralisation.

The first reaction of the directors, as you would expect, was to corner as many Blue Sky shares as we could. Alan Cameron and his sleuths at the ASC will never discover it is us, thanks to a trail of blind trusts in Jersey, Panama, Grand Cayman and Hong Kong. If the ASC ever sends an inspector on our trail, his treatment for jet lag will take even longer than the investigation.

We had soaked up about 15 per cent of Blue Sky (no, don't be silly, we didn't lodge a substantial shareholder notice) at an average of 8c and the shares were now standing around 15c. Whispers were beginning to circulate around the market that for once in Blue Sky's misbegotten career it might have made a genuine discovery.

Sir Mark was still beaming at Spender. Penwiper, our poor but dishonest secretary, took over the running. 'Actually, we found two anomalies, sir,' he said. 'Here's the map.'

He handed over the map of Starving Wombat to Sir Mark. Strictly speaking, Bottle the geologist should have presented it, but he was chary of having his fingerprints on the document.

'Marvellous!' chortled Sir Mark. 'From the intensity of the lines, they look very strong.'

Not only were they strong, but very closely spaced. Unfortunately all this accidental field work had been done during a fortnight when Bottle was drying out in a clinic. He had gone on a terminal bender when he heard that skimpies were being barred from the Kalgoorlie pubs and his delirium tremens is still so bad that he spills all but the last inch of every Teachers we pour him.

He hadn't been capable of focussing again until the morning of the board meeting. We showed him the map just before Sir Mark was due to arrive. After gazing at it for a long time, he said: 'I've seen anomalies that run in a straight line and I've seen anomalies that run parallel, but I have never, *ever* seen two running at right angles to each other.'

Then the blood rose in his eyes as a sudden thought struck him. 'Show me the pastoral map,' he cried.

We dug it out and he examined it carefully, then grunted in horror.

'You've found a metallic area of resistivity all right,' Bottle exploded. 'You've plotted the cocky's bloody boundary fences.'

We all stared at the map. Sure enough, our long, thin anomalies were exactly on the four-strand heavy-gauge fence of the sheep station. It must have contained more iron than Mt Tom Price.

'We must release this to the exchange straight away,' Sir Mark jabbered excitedly. 'I'll bet it will make the shares go for a run, what?'

We might have to do a bit of running ourselves. Meanwhile, we're looking for some wood duck who'll take 15 per cent of Blue Sky at cost.

PIERPONT STRIKES GOLD

Heaven knows, Pierpont is not much of a contributor to Blue Sky Mines board meetings at the best of times, but last month he was definitely below par. The board had injudiciously held its meeting on the morning of September 24 — about five hours after Sydney had won the Olympic Games bid — and your correspondent was suffering from a terminal hangover.

Which was why the directors' meeting opened with Pierpont's lifeless remains propped up against the Andronicus decanter at one end of the board table. Many an experienced undertaker would have been fooled and embalmed your correspondent on sight. He was beyond human sensation, being unable to see or breathe, let alone think. The total absence of these faculties is, of course, an essential qualification for a director, so Pierpont was not feeling any remorse.

He was, however, feeling considerable pain. Judging by his splitting headache, Pierpont at some stage of the night had been scalped by Red Indians. He also appeared to have fractured his left kneecap, and for some reason had a gold medal hanging from a ribbon around his neck.

Even so, he failed to win the Berocca Award for Hangover of the Day, because the standard was exceptionally high. Penwiper had been raging at a party all night and was leaning at least 45 degrees off vertical as he struggled to focus on the minutes.

Spender the accountant had spent the night collecting wagers and his eyes were bloodshot from counting banknotes. Bottle the geologist had gone out with a group of engineers to the Homebush Bay construction site, where the Civil & Civic party had started at midnight and accelerated seriously at 4.30 a.m. A museum curator would have identified him not as living flesh at all, but something dug up from Tutankhamen's tomb. Bottle's normally florid face was ashen and he was making small choking noises. There had already been some talk of putting him on a stretcher and giving him a blood transfusion.

It was a measure of the destruction we had wrought on our intellects that the most sentient person present was our chairman. Sir Mark had been blankly unaware of the Olympics (he still thinks Jesse Owens is part of the American team) and had spent the night slumbering. As a result, he was almost alert.

'You look a trifle haggard, Pierpont,' he observed. 'Where did you spend the night?'

'From the way I feel, it must have been in a concrete mixer,' Pierpont replied.

'Hmmm,' muttered Sir Mark, inspecting the medal on Pierpont's thorax. 'This says you were at the Hotel Inter-Continental. Does that seem likely?'

Memory began to drift back to Pierpont's aching brain. Yes, he had been at the hotel, helping the manager, Wolfgang Grimm, to invoke the Olympic spirit. He could even remember that it had all begun with a combination of champagne and schnapps.

Pierpont winced and poured himself another coffee as Sir Mark opened the meeting. The only item on the agenda was a Mabo claim.

Unlike some unenlightened mining companies, Blue Sky has welcomed the Mabo decision. As soon as the judgment was delivered, we recognised it as a heaven-sent opportunity to dump the Endless Shaft mine.

In the geological lexicon of Blue Sky, the word 'mine' is used in the broad, imaginative sense. Endless Shaft occupies a barren stretch of scrubland almost entirely innocent of mineralisation. There is no hole in the ground, only a few scratches where we have taken surface samples from an isolated low-grade outcrop whenever we wanted to impress investors.

Lately the Stock Exchange has become restive. Some busybody noted that we had spent two decades making announcements about Endless Shaft without anything actually happening. When queried, we said we were an ecologically sensitive company and we're trying not to damage the local flora. That excuse was given two years ago and is now starting to wear thin.

The Official History of Blue Sky Mines

We face the stark alternative of either abandoning the prospect or exploring it, which would mean spending shareholders' money on drill holes instead of directors' lunches. Then Mabo gave us a third option.

No Aboriginal tribe was ever silly enough to try to live on the wasteland at Endless Shaft. The nearest indigenes were the Bandicoot clan, who occasionally went walkabout a couple of hundred miles to the west.

So Bottle contacted the clan and persuaded them (in return for a Land Cruiser) to make a native title claim to Endless Shaft. This would mean that Blue Sky could not risk shareholders' money exploring the prospect while there was a danger that title might be given to the Bandicoots. And if title went to the Bandicoots, Blue Sky could claim compensation from the federal government for the loss of its valuable mine. Anyone who doubted the value of the mine would be shown some drill cores which Bottle has spent the past month salting with gold, platinum, antimony and anything else he could find.

By this time Sir Mark had finished reading the agenda. He looked up, puzzled. 'Have we heard back from the Bandicoot clan yet?' he asked.

Penwiper made a brave attempt to sit upright, nearly slipping beneath the table in the process. He opened and closed his mouth three times before sound finally emerged.

'I'm afraid there's been a hitch,' he croaked. 'Thanks to our support, the Bandicoots look like getting title to the land. But nobody in the tribe wants to go and live there. Instead, they want us to stay there and pay rent.'

The word 'rent' almost gave Spender an apoplectic fit. 'Rent?' he screamed, 'Pay money to someone outside the board? Over my dead body!' As he collapsed back into his seat, clutching his heart, this seemed a distinct possibility.

Confronted with this crisis, Pierpont's brain lurched into first gear. 'Let's renegotiate the deal with the Bandicoots,' he wheezed. 'Let's agree to stay deadlocked on Endless Shaft. In return, Blue Sky will peg a mineral prospect in the Australian Capital Territory. The Bandicoots can then claim native title over that and Canberra as well. As Paul Keating and the High Court are strong supporters of Aboriginal rights, they'll concede immediately and pay rent to the

Bandicoots for the rest of eternity, which will be much better than relying on Blue Sky for rent. And if the Bandicoots agree to this deal, they get to keep the Land Cruiser.'

'Brilliant,' exclaimed Sir Mark. 'Penwiper, call an ambulance for Bottle and tell him to renegotiate the deal when he recovers. Which, from the look of him, will be some time next year.'

He closed the meeting, and your correspondent limped back to his pied-à-terre to seek solace from Mrs Pierpont.

'I'm sorely afflicted, darling,' Pierpont said as he entered. 'My left leg is covered with bruises for some reason.'

'That would be from Pierpont's Bar last night,' she said. 'You were demonstrating the hop, step and jump.'

Just as well it wasn't the pole vault. And at least Pierpont can claim the first gold of the Sydney Olympics.

HOT GRAVEL, WELL SEASONED

Having waited until Sir Mark Time was safely on vacation at his Portsea gin palace, the rest of Blue Sky's geriatric directors had gathered furtively in the office for a secret board meeting.

'Pity it took so long to get the old dunderhead away this year,' grumbled Spender the accountant. 'We've lost a lot of time in this market.'

Pierpont nodded agreement. Where other companies mine the ground, Blue Sky mines the market. So while there is no danger our company will ever turn a shovelful of earth, it is imperative that we should appear to be in the most fashionable current mining areas. This, of course, means we should currently be perceived as fishing for diamonds in Western Australia's Cambridge Gulf.

Pierpont approves of this policy in broad principle as long as nobody expects him to go near the water in question. Cambridge Gulf runs down to Wyndham off the Joseph Bonaparte Gulf. Pierpont has been on each of these gulfs once and on both occasions found he was sharing the area with a cyclone, giving him a jaundiced opinion of the local climate.

The fauna is even more boisterous than the weather. Halfway up the Cambridge Gulf is the entrance to the Ord River. Pierpont has cruised the Ord twice and can testify that, downstream of the dam, it contains the biggest crocodiles he has over seen. And quite a lot of them, particularly as you reach the red mud flats near the Cambridge Gulf and the Wyndham abattoir.

Anyone who wishes to check this point is welcome to ask Mrs Pierpont, who still has vivid memories of a five metre croc we found opposite our campsite.

'How will we go about salting the lease?' asked Penwiper, our poor but dishonest secretary.

'Easy as pie,' replied Bottle the geologist. 'Just dredge up some gravel off one of the river mouths and throw in a handful of rough diamonds.'

'Aren't diamonds supposed to be accompanied by indicator minerals?' asked Pierpont. 'Won't we have to add a dash of chrome diopside or some microdiamonds or something?'

'Not with alluvial diamonds,' explained Bottle. 'Our stones are supposed to have been washed hundreds of kilometres down a Kimberley riverbed. Indicators would have vanished long ago and any industrial grade stones would have abraded away. So we're only going to find gem quality diamonds.'

The real difficulty was finding a claim to salt. The discovery of diamonds by Cambridge Gulf Exploration has sparked a pegging rush around the whole of the Kimberley coastline. That left Blue Sky with three options:
1. overpegging an existing claim;
2. farming into an existing claim; or
3. going further offshore.

Going offshore was unattractive because the water in the Bonaparte Gulf quickly goes to 60 or 65 metres and the cost of dredging rises correspondingly. Not that we are ever going actually to hire a dredge but we would have to do the arithmetical exercise for the sake of the broking firms.

Even the diamond analysts would soon work out that it would be a hopelessly expensive enterprise, not to mention highly speculative. The chances of finding a gem diamond when you are separated from it by 60 metres of rough water and maybe another 20 metres of silt must be about equivalent to the chances of winning a lottery.

Overpegging was attractive because it is cheap but we have tried that tactic rather too frequently in the past, so we reluctantly opted for the honest course and farmed in on an existing prospect. It is more than 100 kilometres from Cambridge's exploration area but that is an advantage because, if our diamonds turn out to he a different colour from theirs, we can claim they are from a different source.

'It would be expensive to hire a dredge and would take ages to get one up there in the cyclone season anyway,' frowned Spender. 'All we really need is someone to go up to our claim, wade out past the low water mark, shovel up a few tonnes of gravel and bring them back to shore with a rough diamond here and there. After all, you only need half a dozen stones to extrapolate an entire mine.'

The thought of wading around the Cambridge Gulf with nothing but a shovel between himself and the local wildlife would have sent Pierpont into a dead faint if he had not kept a strong grip on the Macallan decanter. Bottle, who knows the waters even better, looked at the ceiling. Penwiper said: 'That sounds like fun! And I've never been up north.'

Pierpont heaved a sigh of relief. Company secretaries, after all, are infinitely expendable.

'Good lad!' beamed Bottle. 'You'll find it an unforgettable experience.'

TOTAL QUALITY COMES TO BLUE SKY

Long-suffering shareholders of Blue Sky Mines (No Liability Except At Gunpoint) will be thrilled to know that the company is introducing Total Quality Management. We held a board meeting on the subject just last week.

Our figurehead chairman, Sir Mark Time, was plainly struggling with the concept.

'TQM?' he gruffed uncomprehendingly. 'Isn't that what they use on the Ford production line? And if I remember rightly, they still had to close their Homebush factory.'

Spender gave his accountant's smile, showing just the tips of his teeth. 'Not all aspects of TQM are applicable to a small exploration company such as Blue Sky,' he said. 'In our case, we intend to introduce the latest concepts in information systems and ore reserve estimates.'

The Official History of Blue Sky Mines

'And it sounds good in prospectuses,' added Pierpont.

The spectacle of Sir Mark attempting to think is not a pretty sight. He sat slack-jawed, staring haplessly at Spender for fully a minute before finding speech again.

'Well, all right,' he said. 'But please explain – I'm afraid I haven't the foggiest notion what you're suggesting.'

'Of course, Sir Mark,' beamed Spender, showing about half the bicuspids this time. 'We're making three innovations. The first is in Penwiper's department.'

Penwiper cleared his throat. 'It's the latest concept in information storage,' he said. 'It will streamline all our record keeping. Instead of cluttering our office with filing cabinets containing hard-copy records, we are going to do everything on a whiteboard.'

'What kind of records?' asked Sir Mark.

'Everything,' bubbled Penwiper enthusiastically. 'Minutes of board meetings will be kept on the whiteboard and wiped off as soon as the meeting's over. Exploration data will be written on the whiteboard and wiped off as soon as the statement goes to the stock exchange. There won't be a shred of paper in the office!'

'Er . . . I hate to ask this,' muttered Sir Mark. 'But are you sure that would be legal?'

'It's been endorsed by the highest in the land,' Spender reassured him. 'The Prime Minister has said that there is absolutely nothing wrong with it when the Opposition were up in arms about Ros Kelly keeping departmental records that way.'

'Well, you can't get better support than that,' Sir Mark conceded. 'What else are we doing?'

Bottle the geologist tore himself away from the Macallan decanter to say: 'There have been some important advances in reserve estimation.'

He pointed out recent breakthroughs by two companies which had issued prospectuses for reopening old nickel mines. In valuing their mines, both companies assumed a future nickel price of $US4 a lb, which was double the prevailing price.

The important point here is that in estimating the value of an ore deposit, it is current practice to assume that the future price of the product will be higher than the current price.

'This will be a great benefit,' said Bottle, reaching for the decanter again. 'If we restate the nickel reserves at our Endless Shaft mine at $US4 instead of $US2, it suddenly becomes viable.'

'I thought Endless Shaft was a gold mine,' Sir Mark frowned.

'That was last week,' said Pierpont. 'We need to stay flexible in our thinking in case nickel becomes more fashionable.'

'And there's another innovation in modern thinking,' said Bottle. 'Not only can we assume the price, we can also assume the reserves.'

'Are you sure?' asked Sir Mark, looking more hapless than ever.

'Absolutely,' said Bottle, pouring himself yet another Macallan.

His authority this time was the valuation of Aztec Mining which was used to defend Aztec when that company was fending off an unwelcome takeover bid from Poseidon Gold. Aztec and its independent advisers had totted up the proved and probable reserves of Aztec's mines and valued its net assets at 85c a share.

Then they pushed the valuation up to $1.01 a share on the grounds that Aztec had 'additional potential value of $60 million to $80 million'. This additional potential value depends partly on reserves which have not yet been found at the Bounty gold mine in Western Australia and the Woodcutters zinc mine in the Northern Territory.

Bounty's total proven and probable reserves of 4.8 million tonnes were increased by 800,000 tonnes of indicated additional reserves because its orebodies were open at depth. Endless Shaft's reserves, being imaginary, are even more open so Bottle has presumed we are free to assume extra ore exists also.

'I don't know,' Sir Mark murmured dubiously. 'The ASC has been making some very nasty noises about Blue Sky lately. If we tried to adopt these concepts they might very well investigate us, even though we were able to plead that respectable companies such as Aztec had created a precedent.'

'We'd have the best lawyers in the business on our side,' said Spender. 'The legal adviser to the Aztec statement was Atanaskovic Hartnell.'

Relief flooded over Sir Mark's careworn visage, restoring him as water does a parched flower.

'Oh well, it's all right then!' he exclaimed. 'Silly of me to worry, wasn't it?'

The Macallan decanter being empty, we adjourned for lunch, Penwiper dusting off the whiteboard on the way.

BLUE SKY'S SURPRISE CHRISTMAS PARCEL

This month we celebrate one of the proudest centenaries in Australia's history. One hundred years ago, the Londonderry Gold Mine (Ltd) was floated in London.

For the benefit of those who have forgotten, we'll run over the details. The Londonderry was found 12 miles south of Coolgardie in June 1894 by a bunch of young novice prospectors. It was essentially a rich patch in an otherwise barren quartz reef.

They took some 10,000 ounces from a hole not much bigger than a grave and then sold it to the Earl of Fingall – who was touring the goldfields buying mines at the time – for £180,000 plus a one-sixth interest in the company to be floated.

His Lordship rushed back to London and floated the Londonderry. The company was formed with 700,000 £1 shares, of which

The 1990s and the Recession We Just Had to Have

one-sixth were reserved for the prospectors and another 200,000 were reserved for the promoters and their friends.

The remaining 467,000 shares were sold to the public at £1 each, raising £467,000. Of that, the promoters pocketed £417,000 in preliminary expenses, leaving the Londonderry with just £50,000 working capital.

Note that the mine cost £180,000 but a few weeks later in London the promoters claimed the preliminary expenses totalled £417,000. The difference is £237,000.

Pierpont has often wondered how the Earl and his mates managed to spend that much money in such a short time. It couldn't have been maintenance on the mine, because that had been sealed. Were sub-underwriting commissions a bit high in London in 1894? Did Lord Fingall have to catch an expensive boat home? Did he have to *buy* an expensive boat to get home?

The valuation multiple is interesting, too. A mine which had been sold for £300,000 if we include the vendor shares at par was capitalised at £700,000 in little more time than it took to catch a steamer from Perth to Tilbury. This represents an appreciation of 133 per cent in a few weeks. Or to round it up, about 1,000 per cent per annum.

Lord Fingall justified the valuation by a calculation that the mine would yield gold at a rate of £300,000 a foot. Pedantic historians have since pointed out that when the mine was reopened it was discovered that there was no gold left and everybody did their money except for the vendors, but that of course is irrelevant.

The cardinal principle here, which must never be forgotten, is that mines are not meant for mining. Mines are meant for valuing and for raising money in prospectuses. Subsequent mining only confuses the issue and – in the opinion of Blue Sky's board – should be outlawed as soon as the prospectus is filled.

At Blue Sky we felt something should be done to mark the centenary of the Londonderry, so we are floating the Dying Dingo gold prospect, which we sold years ago but have recently bought back for $500. We are hoping to get $10 million for it in a prospectus coming your way soon.

Great as Pierpont's admiration is for the pioneers, their methodology was sometimes crude. Indeed, their valuations frequently appear to have been conducted on the YGWYG principle (You Get What You Grab).

If the old boys wanted $10 million for Dying Dingo they would have simply flogged the prospectus to the wood ducks, pocketed the money and headed for Brazil. But today, thank heavens, we can do this on a scientific basis.

Now promise you won't tell the ASC but, frankly, Dying Dingo isn't much of a mine. A few old-timers scratched at the deposit. They only went a few feet underground before coming to their senses and quitting, but they turned over just sufficient earth for us to call it a mine rather than a prospect.

It's got just about every problem you can imagine. It's remote. It's low-grade gold. There's not much of it. And there's no water.

And if we had enough water to run a treatment plant we'd really be in trouble. The ore (to use the noun loosely) is accompanied by antimony. The only way of separating the two metals in processing would be by roasting and there's no way the deposit could justify the expense.

Indeed, Bottle the geologist and your correspondent have had some desultory arguments about whether Dying Dingo is a sub-economic gold deposit with antimony impurities or a sub-economic antimony deposit with gold impurities.

The deposit is also contaminated by the presence of low-grade shale which, being carboniferous, would effectively screen the gold from the carbon in the carbon-in-pulp plant (if we were so silly as to build one) with the result that all the gold would go through to the tailings.

Whereas your ordinary board might be disheartened by these factors, at Blue Sky we see them as opportunities. Depending on which is fashionable in the market at the time, we can value Endless Shaft as a gold mine, an antimony mine or a coal mine.

So much for the facts about Dying Dingo. Facts are plodding and tiresome. Let's leave them behind us and waft into the airy fictions of mine valuation.

How do we collect $10 million for Dying Dingo? Originally we tried valuing it by the empirical method. Under the empirical method the first thing you do is to conceive a conceptual target. So we conceived Dying Dingo to be 1 million tonnes at 3 grams, which seemed good round figures. Then we put on a discount factor of 99 per cent — and just as well, because if it was 100 per cent we would have been back where we started. This is, by the way, an actual method of valuing mines.

The calculation was pretty simple: 1,000,000 tonnes multiplied by 3 grams, divided by 31.1 to convert it to ounces, then take one per cent of the figure and multiply by the ruling gold price of $A520 an ounce.

That came out at half a million dollars, which was one-twentieth of what we wanted. Obviously we hadn't tried hard enough at conceiving. We couldn't do much with the conceptual grade, three grams being already about three times what it was, but conceptual tonnage seemed to lend itself to adjustment.

So we reconceived Dying Dingo to be 5 million tonnes at 3 grams and sliced the discount factor to 98 per cent. One percentage point doesn't look very much, but in this case it effectively doubled the orebody and combined with the higher tonnage, had the effect of multiplying the value of Dying Dingo by 10. It was now worth $5 million. Better . . . but we still needed to sharpen our pencils a bit.

When one valuation method doesn't give you the result you need, you try the next. So Blue Sky tried the multiple of exploration expenditure method. This method takes past exploration expenditure and committed future expenditure and multiplies them by a factor called the prospective enhancement multiplier, or PEM, although at Blue Sky we like to think of it as the vendor enhancement multiplier, or VEM.

The multiplier can be anywhere between 5 and 0, but normally tends to hover around 3. This valuation method is based on the theory that the more money other mining companies have spent on a prospect before abandoning it, the more valuable it gets (with an interesting qualification which Pierpont will reveal in a minute).

Future exploration expenditure has an equally interesting philosophical basis. The more you say you are going to spend on a project, the more it is worth. For example, if Blue Sky said it was going to spend a million dollars on a project and applied a multiplier of 0.5 then suddenly the prospect would become worth $500,000.

In Blue Sky's case the future had to be approached delicately because — as usual — the Blue Sky board intends to steal the $10 million and not spend anything on exploration at all.

With past exploration expenditure there was a different problem. According to our most expert advice, the multiplier could not be applied to known past exploration expenditure because that would be taken into account in the purchase price, which in our case was only $500. Only previously unrevealed exploration or confidential exploration was therefore eligible for the multiplier. So we needed to discover exploration that was previously unknown.

The solution seemed obvious. This was clearly a case for forgery. Create a few records from the 1930s. Our poor but dishonest secretary Penwiper has been forging the signature of Sir Mark Time for years. He welcomed this chance to diversify and it would have been valuable training for him before we moved him up to the big time next year and got him to do the audit certificate. But unfortunately, we couldn't get any paper that was the right age.

So we moved to Plan B. We discovered an old prospector who now lives on a park bench at Cottesloe and got him to sign a certificate saying he had done a million dollars worth of exploration at Dying Dingo. The going rate for his signature — if any other company promoters are interested — is two bottles of fruity sweet sherry.

With our million dollars of previously unknown prior expenditure (any more would have looked suspicious), we applied the top multiplier of 5 and still came up with only $5 million.

It was at that stage we remembered two recent prospectuses had established the important principle that we could also assume a future price for the commodity. In those prospectuses, the valuation of orebodies had been assisted considerably by assuming that the price of nickel was going to double.

Our troubles were over. The prospectus for Endless Shaft, due out in the Christmas party season when investors' critical faculties are low or non-existent, will assume a doubling of the gold price. Whether this will be achieved by a future rise in the Comex price, a future fall in the $A is a matter of keen debate between Spender and Bottle. Pierpont favours a combination of both, and this compromise solution will probably prevail.

The 1990s and the Recession We Just Had to Have

So Dying Dingo, which we bought a few months ago for $500 (a figure you will not find anywhere in the prospectus) will be sold to the wood ducks (sorry, slip of the quill there – Pierpont should have said the investing public) for $10 million. A figure supported by both the empirical method and the multiple of exploration expenditure method, combined with permissible assumptions about the future price of the commodity.

Admittedly there are rather a lot of assumptions around. We have assumed a tonnage, assumed a grade, assumed a multiplier, assumed a discount factor and assumed a future commodity price. But all are justified by precedent in prospectuses for which nobody was jailed or even queried.

And best of all, we are maintaining a great Australian tradition.

BACKGROUNDER

INSIDE THE CROESUS CLUB

The architecture of the original Croesus Club was Georgian, the old place having been put together in the days when the monarchy still gloried in the name of Hanover. If it were still around today, it would be in grave danger of sinking under the weight of preservation orders slapped on it by well-meaning conservationists.

The geriatric brigands of the club, however, scented the breeze in the late 1960s – almost the last time we could commit some atrocity on our architectural heritage (Goldfields House and the first AMP headquarters at Circular Quay come to mind). So we used our historic links with the Liberals controlling the city council to get building permission, raised some funds with a debenture issue to club members and smacked up a 20-storey building on the site.

The exterior of the new building is awful. We chose the typical design of the day – an up-ended glass matchbox relieved by a few perfunctory concrete mullions.

This was for three reasons: (1) it was cheap, being drawn with a T-square and ruler one wet Saturday by an architectural student who happened to be Pierpont's grandson; (2) a more elaborate design would have taken longer and we had to get it up while Jack Mundey wasn't looking; and (3) as it has no aesthetic value we can tear it down any time we like and replace it with a 60-storey block.

Meanwhile, we have let the top 18 floors to a bank and a life office and are comfortably ensconced in the bottom two floors while growing very wealthy on rent escalations.

All that has been lost is the facade of the old club. The inner skin was retained intact except for the north-eastern corner where we had to install a doorway and lift bank for the tenants. Being in the heart of the CBD (given the nature of the members, the club has to be within tottering distance of the Stock Exchange) the building is now frightfully valuable and attracts premium rents.

The decision to retain the two bottom floors was taken deliberately. It enabled us to retain the inner shell of the club intact without missing a single Bollinger while the construction was in

The 1990s and the Recession We Just Had to Have

progress. Also, the low plot ratio was originally chosen with the purpose of discouraging members from jumping off the window ledges during market crashes. Over the years this has saved the life of many a depressed member, notably when Mainline hit the wall in '74.

The entrance portal is deliberately unobtrusive and unattractive, the main feature being the mustachioed porter. This chap, usually a retired sergeant-major, has three vital tasks. The first is to guide any lost soul gently but firmly out again. Visitors and guests are not permitted in the club. His second purpose is to mind members' umbrellas and his third is to answer the club's only telephone.

Members of the Croesus Club are by no means persuaded that the telephone was invented by Alexander Graham Bell. They are convinced it is the personal invention of the Devil and refuse to allow its clangorous presence in their midst, signalling the advent of wives, insurance salesmen, bailiffs and other scourges.

Nor do we have any other Telecom or landlines bearing such services as Reuters. These estimable news services and bits of software tell you what has just happened. At the Croesus Club our aim is to create the happenings. As Noel Coward said of television: 'It isn't for watching – it's for appearing on.'

Past the porter's desk a right turn takes you into the main lobby, decorated with trophies of the Sudan contingent, and up the magnificent native cedar staircase to the top floor.

The entire top floor is given over to just two rooms, the Jim Fisk Bar and the dining room. For the benefit of those unacquainted with financial history, the bar is named after our hero.

Jim Fisk and Jay Gould were great operators in American railway stocks in the 19th century. Their classic battle was for control of the Erie, when they had possession of the company but Commodore Vanderbilt was trying to take them over in an on-market raid. Every time the Commodore bought 51 per cent of the company, Jim and Jay would print more share certificates and sell them to him. The printing press was rightly perceived as the Erie's main asset and kept under armed guard in the cellar. Since then the laws on issued capital have changed a bit, but Pierpont passes on the tactic to BHP in case they ever have more trouble with the likes of Robert Holmes à Court.

The dining room has only large tables. It is not possible to reserve, nor to have an intimate lunch for two. This is a club. There is a long table on the western wall bearing game pie, jugged hare, salads and so forth. A short menu of hot dishes is available daily for anyone who wants the crayfish thermidor or the roast pheasant.

Pierpont has always been proud of the Croesus Club dining room, but he has seen one club with more panache. That was the time he supped at the Oxford and Cambridge Club in The Mall, where the dining room had an exceedingly high ceiling and the windows were swagged with drapes. Pierpont was gazing at the drapes – made from heavy cloth in a dusty red colour – when his host drawled: 'Uniform cloth for the French Army, you know. Some of our chaps managed to loot the baggage train at Waterloo.'

The Croesus club can't match that, but Pierpont doubts whether any other club can either.

The ground floor at the Croesus Club behind the staircase comprises a series of smaller rooms. The largest of these is the library, lined with books and dotted with chesterfield leather chairs. Pierpont has never yet seen any member, sober or otherwise, ever take a book from one of the shelves. They help themselves liberally to the daily papers, which after a few usages open automatically at the share quotations. Before noon the library is marked by cathedral silence, but after dessert the snoring is apt to be obtrusive.

If you are a late luncher and arrive at the library to find all of the chairs occupied, the best alternative is the trophy room just across the corridor. Here, if you are not bothered by the heads of stuffed moose and leopards, one can find a bit of peace after a strenuous lunch. Pierpont often enjoys a brandy here before stubbing his Davidoff corona in the elephant's foot ashtray.

If he is feeling active, your correspondent might spend the afternoon in the billiards room at the rear of the ground floor. This has been the scene for many a happy hour for your correspondent as he racked up nursery cannons against Leo Liability the stockbroker while planning a market raid. A small glass case in one corner preserves Essington Lewis' marker chalk.

The other room at the rear is the games room, normally not occupied until the evening when those who are still too sober to go home and face their wives will assemble for a hand of poker. Unless you are used to wagering on the scale of John Spalvins, Pierpont does not recommend this school. Your correspondent once lost a small oil refinery on four sevens.

The 1990s and the Recession We Just Had to Have

On Friday nights this room is a source of no little hardship to the staff, because the club rules are that the club closes only when the last member leaves.

You will probably find Pierpont there come midnight this evening, smoking a Ramon Allones and dealing five-card blind. According to all the actuaries your correspondent died some time in 1973, so while he's working on borrowed time Pierpont reckons he might as well enjoy it.

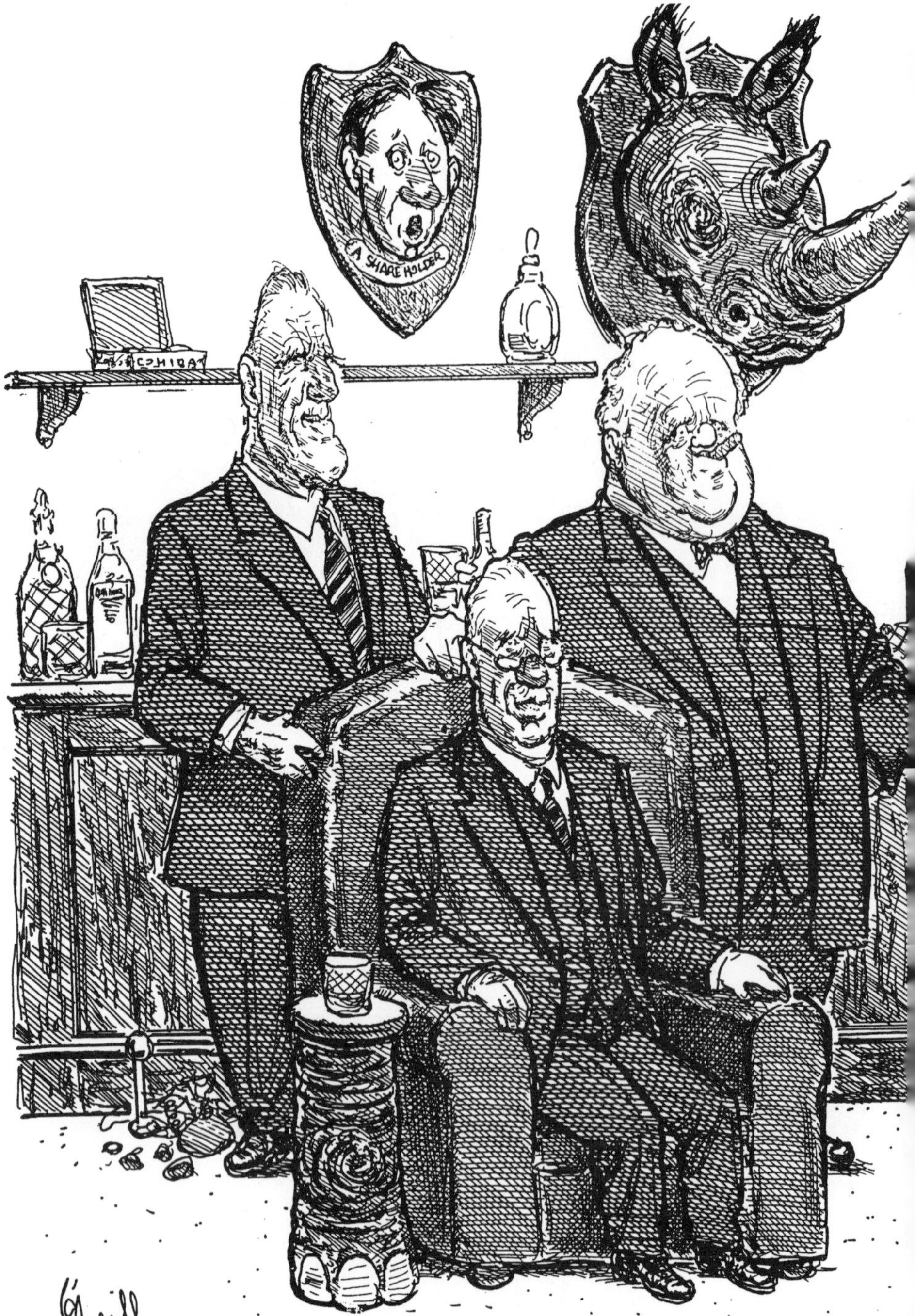
A SHARE HOLDER
COHIBA
O'Neill

BUSINESS
PROMISING TUNGSTEN GRADES
DIRECTORS OPTIMISTIC
STOP PRESS
LAST CARD CALL
Jim Fisk